The planning and management of environmentally sensitive areas

THEMES IN RESOURCE MANAGEMENT
Edited by Professor Bruce Mitchell, University of Waterloo

PAUL F. J. EAGLES

The planning and management of environmentally sensitive areas

Longman
London and New York

Longman Group Limited
Longman House, Burnt Mill, Harlow
Essex CM20 2JE, England
Associated companies throughout the world

Published in the United States of America
by Longman Inc., New York

First published 1984

British Library Cataloguing in Publication Data
Eagles, Paul F. J.
    The planning and management of environmentally
    sensitive areas. – (Themes in resource management)
    1. City planning   2. Regional planning
    I. Title   II. Series
    711   HT166

ISBN 0-582-30074-6

Library of Congress Cataloging in Publication Data
Eagles, Paul F. J., 1949–
    The planning and management of environmentally
    sensitive areas.
    (Themes in resource management)
    Bibliography: p.
    Includes index.
    1. Nature conservation.   2. Regional planning.
    3. Conservation of natural resources.   4. Environmental
    policy.   I. Title.   II. Series.
    QH75.E23   1984   333.95   83-13645
    ISBN 0-582-30074-6

Printed in Hong Kong by
Wing Lee Printing Co Ltd

Contents

v

Contents

List of figures

List of figures

List of tables

Acknowledgements

This has been a difficult book to write. So much of the material used is 'fugitive' literature in the form of plans, briefs and policy statements that are unpublished in the normal sense of the word. Many thanks must go to the planners in the case-study municipalities who helped dig up and interpret those parts of their plans that were of interest to me. I hope that my interpretations do justice to the work of these individuals who are so much in the front line of conservation.

I would like to acknowledge the help of my wife Catherine and my three sons Russell, Ryan and Robert, who have become used to the fact that their husband and father has been frequently closeted in his den for long periods of time in recent years. Hopefully, I can make it up to them by planning outdoor explorations of some of the lovely natural environments that exist near our home.

Special thanks must go to Dr George Francis of the Department of Man-Environment Studies of the University of Waterloo who started me on the explorations in this field that ultimately led to a doctoral dissertation on the subject and to this book. Dr Robert Dorney of the School of Urban and Regional Planning at the University of Waterloo is the dean of environmental management in Canada. He supervised the thesis research and has continued to provide thoughtful leadership on many aspects of the field. Dr Bruce Mitchell is the careful editor who has stimulated the writing of this book. Ms Jane Steele typed the entire manuscript on to the excellent word processing system at the University of Waterloo. Mr Ed Poropat contributed the excellent wildlife drawings. No man is an island and the following acknowledgements reveal clearly that a work such as this is influenced by and dependent on so many. Thanks to all those who provided assistance.

Mr P. Attack, Senior Planner, Regional Municipality of Halton, Oakville, Ontario, Canada. Dr R. Dorney, Professor, School of Urban and Regional Planning, University of Waterloo, Waterloo, Ontario, Canada. Dr G. Francis, Professor, Department of Man-Environment Studies, University of Waterloo, Waterloo, Ontario, Canada. Mr J. D. Hall, Manager of Resource Planning for Halton Region Conservation Authority, Milton, Ontario. Mr O. Ikenouye, Chairman, National Parks Association of Japan, Tokyo, Japan. Mr T. Itoh, graduate student, Kyoto University, Kyoto, Japan. Dr J. Levy, Associate Professor, Department of Recreation, University of Waterloo, Waterloo, Ontario, Canada. Ms R. A. Menyes, Manager of Resource Planning, Credit Valley Conservation Authority, Meadowvale, Ontario, Canada. Mr T. Mori, Parks and Recreation Foundation of Japan, Tokyo, Japan. Dr G. Nelson, Dean, Faculty of Environmental Studies, University of Waterloo, Waterloo, Ontario, Canada. Mr C. Patterson, graduate student, School of Landscape Architecture, University of Guelph, Ontario, Canada. Mr G. Probert, County Planning Officer, Gwent County Council, Cwmbran, Wales. Dr A. Sato, President, Parks and Open Space Association of Japan, Tokyo, Japan. Mr T. F. Sprott, Director of Physical Planning, Grampian Regional Council, Aberdeen, Scotland. Mr R. E. Tustian, Planning Director, Montgomery County, Maryland-National Capital Park and Planning Commission, Silver Spring, Maryland, United States. Mr M. Watkins, Assistant Regional Officer, Nature Conservancy Council, Cardiff, Wales.

We are indebted to the following for permission to reproduce copyright material:

American Association for the Advancement of Science for our Table 2.1 from fig in 'The Strategy of Ecosystem Development' E. P. Odum *Science* Vol 164, 18.4.69, pp 262–270. Copyright 1969 by AAAS; the Editor, American Journal of Agricultural Economics for an extract from (Bishop 1978); the author, G. Argus for our fig 4.1 (Argus & White 1982); The Canadian Society of Landscape Architects, Owen Scott & Assoc. Ltd & the author, Dr. R. S. Dorney for our Table 5.3 (Dorney 1977b); Elsevier Scientific Publishing Co & the authors, R. Dorney & D. Hoffman for our Table 2.2 (Dorney 1977b & Dorney & Hoffman 1979); the Editor, Florida State University Law Review for extracts from (DiRista 1982); the author, D. A. Goode for our fig 6.2 (Goode (undated) & Goode 1981); Biological Records Centre of the Institute of Terrestial Ecology for our fig 6.1 (International Bee Research Association); International Union for Conservation of Nature & Nature Reserves for an extract from p 13 *United Nations List of Natural Parks and Equivalent Reserves* 2nd ed. 1971; the author, Ian MacNaughton for extracts from p iii (MacNaughton 1971); Maryland National Capital Park and Planning Commission for fig 6.16; the author, Dr. Gordon Nelson for an extract from p 48 (Nelson 1978); Niagara Escarpment Commission for fig 6.13; T & A. D. Poyser, Calton for our fig 4.2 from pp 168–9 (Sharrock 1976); the author, Richard Tustian for an extract from letter 22.1082 to Dr. Paul F. J. Eagles; University of Wisconsin for an extract from p 573 (Kelso 1976).

Foreword

The Themes in Resource Management series has several objectives. One is to identify and to examine substantive and enduring resource management and development problems. Attention will range from local to international scales, from developed to developing nations, from the public to the private sector, and from biophysical to political considerations.

A second objective is to assess responses to these management and development problems in a variety of world regions. Several responses are of particular interest: *research* and *action programmes*. The former involves the different types of analysis which have been generated by natural resource problems. The series will assess the kinds of problems being defined by investigators, the nature and adequacy of evidence being assembled, the kinds of interpretations and arguments being presented, the contributions to improving theoretical understanding as well as resolving pressing problems, and the areas in which progress and frustration are being experienced. The latter response involves the policies, programmes and projects being conceived and implemented to tackle complex and difficult problems. The series is concerned with reviewing their adequacy and effectiveness.

A third objective is to explore the way in which resource analysis, management and development might be made more complementary to one another. Too often analysts and managers go their separate ways. A good part of the blame for this situation must lie with the analysts who too frequently ignore or neglect the concerns of managers, unduly emphasize method and technique, and exclude explicit consideration of the managerial implications of their research. It is hoped that this series will demonstrate that research and analysis can contribute both to development of theory and to resolution of important societal problems.

While hazard lands are areas from which man must be protected, environmentally sensitive areas are landscapes that must be protected from man. Paul Eagles' book on environmentally sensitive areas – defined as ecosys-

tems whose natural characteristics and processes are to be maintained, preserved and protected – touches upon all the objectives in the series. He
reviews concepts from fields as diverse as ecology, economics and law to
assess their utility for managing environmentally sensitive areas. The book
considers pertinent theory, presents a planning and management strategy,
develops general and site planning guidelines, and provides four case studies. These detailed examples are drawn from Great Britain, Japan, Canada
and the United States.

A striking feature is the focus upon the municipal or local government
role in the management of natural areas. Conservation and environmental
management is usually associated with state/provincial or national levels of
government, or even with international levels such as the Man and Biosphere or World Conservation Strategy programmes of the United Nations.
Nevertheless, Eagles convincingly argues that it is local government that is
in the front line of resource allocation and management decisions, and that
it will complement efforts at other levels if the task is done well there. At
whichever level attention is directed to the protection of environmentally
sensitive areas, the objectives are similar to those established by the World
Conservation Strategy in 1980: to maintain essential ecological processes and
life-support systems, to preserve genetic diversity, and to ensure the sustainable utilization of species and ecosystems.

Paul Eagles is well suited to write this book. He has an undergraduate
degree in biology and graduate degrees in zoology and urban and regional
planning. As an academic, his research has focused upon environmentally
sensitive area management, ranging from supervising inventories of areas to
assessing institutional and administrative arrangements. As a consultant, he
is involved with a firm which offers services in the fields of urban, environmental, development and resource planning. As a private citizen, he has
been the driving force in an advisory group providing ecological and environmental advice to a regional government in Ontario. Thus, he has experience in environmentally sensitive area management as academic researcher,
consultant and citizen. These perspectives are all pertinent to the matters
addressed in this book.

Bruce Mitchell
University of Waterloo
Waterloo, Ontario

February 1983

Preface

The protection of ecological and landscape diversity is a major aim of the conservation movement. Traditionally this has involved the careful management of large blocks of land in national parks by the federal authorities and in provincial or state parks by this lower governmental level. In recent decades environmental managers have begun to realize the need for the development of policy tools for the use of municipal governments, which in themselves have a very important role to play in landscape management.

In this book the planning and management of Environmentally Sensitive Areas by municipal governments are discussed. The relevant theories of environmental management, island biogeography, economics, technology, law and societal attitudes are presented to serve as a basis for the understanding of natural areas and their planning.

Four case studies are presented to give an idea of the policy structure that has developed in a number of countries. Great Britain and Japan are old, stable countries with centuries of institutional experience in land-use management. The County of Gwent in Wales and the Wakayama Prefecture on Honshu have been used for the case studies. Canada and the United States are comparatively young, but are similarly stable politically. Their large size and more recent traditions provide interesting contrasts to the older countries. Halton County in Ontario and Montgomery County in Maryland are the sites of the two North American case studies.

The planning and management of Environmentally Sensitive Areas by municipal governments is taking place in each of the four countries discussed in detail and in most of northern Europe and Scandinavia as well. This policy thrust has not been generally recognized to be as wide and sophisticated as it really is.

CHAPTER 1

Introduction

The purpose of the book

The large and continuing increase in the human population and the associated land development is causing widespread alterations in the world's natural ecological systems. Burgeoning human numbers are making increasing demands on the biosphere for all the products which it provides. Larger portions of the energy flow in many ecosystems are being diverted into human consumption with the consistent loss of upper trophic levels in the food webs. Nutrient cycles are being extensively altered, some being enriched, some displaced, some reduced. Overall ecological diversity is decreasing in both a species and structural sense. Species extinction is increasing at an exponential rate and much of it is due to the loss of highly evolved, specialized creatures that cannot survive man-caused environmental change. At the same time, hardy generalist species are often doing very well, sometimes to the scale of assuming pest status. World-wide the natural ecological communities are being utilized, modified and replaced so as to feed man's voracious consumptive needs (Fig. 1.1). In the most densely populated portions of Europe, Asia and North America less than 10 per cent of the natural, terrestrial ecosystems remain in some semblance of their natural state (Fig. 1.2).

These trends threaten the ecosystem on which we all depend for food, fuel and fibre. They have the potential of causing major and irreversible ecological changes. Slowly, over time, an interesting and positive set of resource management institutions has been developing in an effort to deflect or stem this tide. The last two decades have seen the largest and most rapid activity. These institutions now include: the establishment of national, provincial and local parks; the protection of endangered species; the establishment and enforcement of limits for the taking of wildlife by hunting or fishing; the use of sustained yield forestry and soil conservation practices in agriculture; the limitation of pollution from industrial and residential point sources; the

1

Figure 1.1 Housing construction in Cambridge, Ontario. Typical urban development results in the complete removal of terrestrial ecosystems. The woods on the horizon will be saved as a city-owned park.

Figure 1.2 Residential lot development in Myrtle Beach, South Carolina. Intensive recreational pressures along the Atlantic seaboard have resulted in large-scale residential developments. Here a pine forest is being cut prior to lot sale.

development of sewage collection and treatment systems; the development of water management programmes including water quality and flood limitations; and the use of environmental impact assessment. Correspondingly, there has been a slow evolution of a number of educational institutions that can produce a cadre of professionals with the requisite planning and management skills.

Throughout the world local governments are in the forefront of land use allocation. Daily they make decisions which affect the quality of the environment. Traditionally, environmental management has been the concern of senior levels of government only. Do municipalities recognize the role that they can play in the planning and management of natural ecosystems? Have they the capability to develop and implement the appropriate policies? What have they done up to now? This book explores these components of the planning and management of natural ecological communities by local municipal governments.

Why protect Environmentally Sensitive Areas? There are two basic reasons. The first is essentially utilitarian. These areas contain processes and products that are useful to man now and in the future. This environmental capital is a resource bank that will continue to be of use, often in unforeseen ways, for the indefinite future. The second is altruistic and moralistic. Nature deserves to survive because it is. Each species has a right to exist. The first reason is the more pragmatic and the one that provides a stronger justification for natural area protection. The ecological functions and human uses of natural areas are large in number. A few of the most important are shown in Table 1.1.

The World Conservation Strategy outlines a world-wide policy thrust for conservation (IUCN 1980). The major environmental aims include:

1. The conservation of the world's living resources in order to support a long-term sustainable level of development.
2. The maintenance of essential ecological processes and life-support systems.
3. The preservation of genetic diversity.
4. The sustainable utilization of species and ecosystems.

The major planning and management issues include:

1. The development of national and subnational conservation strategies.
2. The development of policy-making and management institutions that are capable of integrating conservation and development.
3. The development of rational resource allocation and environmental planning institutions and the associated legislative and administrative arrangements.
4. The improvement of research and management training functions so as to facilitate sustainable development.
5. The education and the participation of the public in conservation issues.

Table 1.1 Ecological functions and human uses of ESAs

Environmentally Sensitive Areas are important, useful and sensitive features of the landscape that need to be protected. They provide long-term benefit to the biosphere in total and to the human society which depends on the products which the biosphere provides. A few of the ecological functions and human uses of ESAs are listed below.

1. Protection of gene pools for the future. The later uses could include: reclamation of derelict lands, breeding of genes into commercial species or development of new commercial products such as antibiotics.
2. Protection of rare or endangered species and their habitat.
3. Provision of travel corridors and resting places for migratory species.
4. Preservation of mature, stable climax ecosystems with their constituent complete food webs and trophic level complexity.
5. Serving the purpose of benchmarks to which all disturbed areas can be compared.
6. Conservation of large blocks of habitat for species, especially upper trophic level predators, that require extensive areas for breeding and survival.
7. Protection of areas for the nesting or breeding of colonial species, such as herons, terns or many fish species.
8. Protection of representative samples of different ecotones or community types within an existing biogeographical province.
9. Allowance for ecological succession to continue unhindered.
10. Protection of areas for the breeding of wildlife that require undisturbed natural areas.
11. Conservation of areas with relatively complete nutrient recycling processes and normal energy flows.
12. For the study of the population dynamics of any or all constituent species.
13. For the study of predator/prey and parasite/host relationships in areas with natural food-chain processes.
14. Protection of paleobotanical resources for the study of past environments and their change over time.
15. To serve groundwater recharge, low stream flow augmentation, flood peak reduction and headwater protection functions for the hydrological system.
16. Filtration and cleaning of air and water flows. Almost all sewage treatment is dependent upon the natural ecosystems to complete the treatment process.
17. Reduction of soil erosion.
18. Protection of unique geological features that show significant glacial, fluvial, depositional or erosional processes.
19. Limitation of construction on hazardous lands such as floodplains, steep slopes or unstable soils.
20. Provision of areas for public education of resources and their management.
21. Protection of aesthetically pleasing environments.
22. To provide sources of commercial products such as outdoor recreation.

These elements of the strategy are primarily aimed at world-wide and national concerns. The protection and management of local Environmentally Sensitive Areas by municipal governments can fulfil part of these conservation needs. Local natural areas serve a role in conserving living resources. They help protect genetic diversity and help maintain essential ecological processes. They are important benchmarks that can be used to establish sustainable levels of resource utilization. These local areas could be a vital component of any international-national-state-local hierarchy of conservation activity. Many of the upper-level efforts would be unnecessary if all the local conservation efforts were successful.

The preservation of natural ecological diversity has long been a concern of the conservation movement in many countries. The major policy tools that have been developed include the protection of individual natural areas by park designation, and the application of fish and game laws.

Since the early 1960s, the development of the ecological philosophy and its applied counterpart, environmental management, has established a fundamental and important change in the approach to environmental issues. The most basic element has been the development of public policies and programmes using a broad systems approach based upon an increasingly sophisticated ecological understanding of landscape productivity, processes and dynamics. Furthermore, there has been a better appreciation of the importance of 'scale', by which is meant the hierarchical relationship of environmental issues from continental to local in size and importance. At the same time the environmental managers have begun to realize that a knowledge of public policy-making institutions is vital if the necessary structural changes are to be implemented. In other words, they have become professionally political.

Traditionally the protection of ecological diversity through the protection of natural areas has been dealt with only at senior levels of government. The important role of the planning and land management functions of the various municipal governments with regard to environmental quality is starting to be recognized. Action to establish a variety of environmental management tools that can be used at the municipal level has been started. One of these tools has been the establishment of Environmentally Sensitive Area (ESA) policies in an effort to protect the smaller scale but important natural areas in a municipality.

The ecological diversity of the biosphere and the related natural landscapes can be considered to be common property for the use of all citizens in both the present and the future (Fig. 1.3). The ability of the individual in society to influence decision-making processes that affect common property is the important concern of any discussion concerning public participation. The attitudes of society towards natural ecosystems are part of the decision-making matrix in all countries and must be considered before plans can be developed or implemented.

Theory provides a device for the creation of a coherent understanding from a number of diverse elements or phenomena. In this book the theoretical elements that are seen to have the most forceful impact upon natural area planning are those that deal with: planning, ecology, island biogeography, environmental planning, public participation, economics, and the

Figure 1.3 A mature deciduous forest.   Mature ecological communities are becoming relatively rare due to extensive landscape alteration.

economics of natural environments. The experiences of others in environmental management, the regulation of common property, natural area planning and ESA planning, along with theoretical considerations, provide a base for the analysis of the situations in various countries.

This book has a basic tenet of ecological determinism which can be defined as:

> A particular point of view in planning which advocates that retention of natural elements and processes should be given priority in planning. Natural elements (such as aquifers, wildlife breeding areas, and floodplains) which are valued by segments of society or freely perform necessary life support or quality of life functions, or whose alteration will significantly damage other valued resources, should be protected on plans and in plan policies (Schwartz *et al.* 1976, p. 64).

Definitions of terms

There are a large number of terms that describe a natural area, park or wildland. One term widely used in conservation approaches, as opposed to recreation, is natural area. A definition of a natural area is:

> An area of land or water which either retains or has reestablished its natural character, although it need not be completely undisturbed, or

which retains unusual flora, fauna, geological or similar features of scientific or educational interest (Nature Conservancy 1975, p. 3).

A nature preserve is:

A natural area which has been dedicated or committed as such, in what is intended to be permanent status, by a governmental, corporate or private owner (Lindsey *et al.* 1969, p. 7).

A park is a specialized area that must fulfil two basic purposes: the protection of a natural resource and the provision of outdoor recreation. Every park planner and every park manager must make difficult decisions on the degree of emphasis that should be placed on each purpose. Inappropriate or excessive recreational uses can degrade natural ecosystems. Conversely, the political justification for the establishment of many parks depends upon human use in the form of recreation. The amount of this use varies from low in nature reserves to high in recreation parks.

The best protected and most visible parks in many countries are those established by the national government. Those established upon the North American model tend to be large and given a high degree of protection. The international definition of a national park is:

a relatively large area (1) where one or several ecosystems are not materially altered by human exploitation and occupation, where plant and animal species, geomorphological sites and habitats are of special scientific, educative and recreative interest or which contains a natural landscape of great beauty and (2) where the highest competent authority of the country has taken steps to prevent or to eliminate as soon as possible exploitation or occupation in the whole area and to enforce effectively the respect of ecological, geomorphological or aesthetic features which led to its establishment and (3) where visitors are allowed to enter, under special conditions, for inspirational, educative, cultural and recreative purposes (IUCN 1971, p. 13).

Large, federated countries also tend to have provincial or state park systems. These vary widely in the size and scale of the parks but some are very extensive. For example, the systems in several Canadian provinces contain parks that fulfil the IUCN definition in all respects except they are not federally managed.

Many countries have local county or city park systems. These tend to be small and dedicated to heavy levels of recreational use.

Over time there has developed an extensive range of terms to describe reserve programmes in a variety of countries. Different programmes have different political environments. Each unit develops its own dynamic balance between the demands of resource protection and resource use. Some of the common terms used in the literature include:

Natural Area (Indiana) (Lindsey *et al.* 1969)
Nature Reserve (Indiana) (Lindsey *et al.* 1969)
Conservation Area (Great Britain) (Stamp 1969)
Federal Research Natural Area (USA) (Franklin *et al.* 1972)
National Nature Reserve (Great Britain) (Sheail 1976)
Local Nature Reserve (Great Britain) (Sheail 1976)
Forest Nature Reserve (Great Britain) (Sheail 1976)
Biosphere Reserve (International) (Batisse 1971)
Natural Reserve (International) (Diamond 1975)
Biotic Natural Area (Wisconsin) (Tans 1974)
Site of Special Scientific Interest (Great Britain) (Nature Conservancy 1975b)
Ecological Reserve (British Columbia) (Department of Lands, Forests and Water Resources 1975)
Environmentally Sensitive Area (Ontario) (Francis and Eagles 1975)
Nature Sanctuary (Hamilton Naturalists Club) (Shivas 1974)
National Park (International) (IUCN 1971)
National Nature Monument (Iran) (Harrington 1977)
Protected Area (Iran) (Harrington 1977)
Wilderness Area (Ontario) (Revised Statutes of Ontario 1970a)
Wildlife Management Area (Ontario) (MNR 1974)
Provincial Park (Ontario) (Revised Statutes of Ontario 1970b)
State Park (New York) (New York State 1976)
Biogenetic Reserve (Europe) (Baum 1976)
Prefectural Natural Parks (Japan) (Japan Environment Agency 1977).

An Environmentally Sensitive Area (ESA) is a specifically bounded land-scape that fulfils one or more of a set of criteria. ESAs are natural landscapes that contain features such as: aquifer recharge, headwaters, unusual plants, wildlife or landforms, breeding or overwintering animal habitats, vital ecological functions, rare or endangered species, or combinations of habitat and landform which could be valuable for scientific research or conservation education. These ESAs may or may not have been significantly affected by certain human activities and they may or may not require intensive manage-ment in order to restore, maintain or improve certain of their natural values. The criteria are presented and discussed in detail in Chapter 4.

In a municipal plan the words Environmentally Sensitive Area give recognition that the area contains an ecosystem whose natural characteristics and processes should be maintained, preserved and protected. Some areas contain geological or physiographic features that are important irrespective of the biological features.

Hazard lands are landscape areas which can be harmful to man and/or his structures and are caused by forces extraneous to him (Schwartz *et al.* 1976). Often, ESAs are found on lands that can be considered to be hazardous, such as those with steep slopes or unstable soils. However, not all hazard lands are ESAs. In general terms, Environmentally Sensitive Areas are those landscapes that must be protected from man while hazard lands are areas from which man must be protected.

Ecology is that branch of science concerned with:

> the interrelationships of organisms and their cycles and rhythms, community development and environments – especially as manifested by natural structure, interaction between different kinds of organisms, geographic distributions, and population alternations (Schwartz *et al.* 1976, p. 66).

The evolving environmental management strategies and institutions are an attempt to provide cultural limitations to human environmental exploitation. In the absence of these societal institutions the environmental degradation will ultimately cause resource limitations to develop.

CHAPTER 2

Environmentally sensitive area planning theory

Introduction

One of the important elements in the development of environmental management in the last 20 years is its basis on a solid, and rapidly evolving, theoretical base. Our understanding of ecology has come to a stage where broad generalizations are now possible. We often can make reasonable predictions of the environmental impacts of our activities. We now better understand how the system works and where we fit in. Much remains to be learned but the field is at a stage where the theory and the associated analytical models can stand up to the scrutiny of those segments of society that are prone to attack environmental concerns.

Specifically, island biogeography, ecological theory and environmental planning theory and the developing field of environmental management have direct relevance to natural area planning and management. The derived principles from ecology provide a theoretical base for the need, the function and the management of ESAs.

Ecological planning theory

Ecological theory

Ecologists, in the sense of natural system scientists, think of ecosystems as being composed of three components (matter, energy and information) interacting in time and space (Richardson and McEvoy 1976). The information is contained primarily in the genetic codes, in the learned or conditioned behaviour of the organisms, and in the organization of the individuals and populations making up the community. Ecologists account for the phenomena that they observe by reference to the three basic factors of matter, energy and information.

Human systems can also be thought of as composed of interactions of matter, energy and information in time and space. The major difference between human and non-human systems is that human systems have developed information storage and processing procedures which are sometimes described as culture (Richardson and McEvoy 1976). These rapidly developing information systems are an emergent property of man which is superimposed upon his biological nature, much as his biological nature is superimposed upon his physical and chemical natures.

Individual organisms contain two kinds of information: that encoded in their genetic code and that encoded as learned behaviour after birth. The genetic information is transmitted from parents to offspring through the DNA, and in a few cases through RNA. However, cultural information is not transferred genetically. The human information storage systems have developed to the stage where the cultural information can be stored and upgraded quickly. Therefore, cultural evolution can proceed at a much faster rate than biological evolution (Richardson and McEvoy 1976).

There is no definite limit to the amount of information available in the universe. Practical limits are set by the mechanisms and resources available for discovering, interpreting and storing the information. Generally, the trend of biological evolution has been towards an increase or continual accumulation of information in the ecosystem. In that context, evolution can be viewed as a learning process which incorporates more information into population systems (Duncan 1976). The development of rapid cultural evolution, which essentially entails the accumulation of information, could be seen as the extrapolation of the information storage trend in biological evolution. This cultural development of man and the strength of his science in developing information has given him power over human and non-human systems (Andreski 1972). Man makes extensive nonbiological manipulation of energy and matter, with tools and machinery, an important part of his adaptive equipment (Richardson and McEvoy 1976). Man's uses of material, energy and information parallel those used by preceding and associated forms of life. It must also be recognized that technology has developed systems that lack any clear counterpart on the nonhuman level. Refinement of inorganic ores, generation of electricity, and the printing of books are examples of three types of flow which are intelligible only in the context of technological systems and not merely as adjuncts to organic systems (Duncan 1976).

Technology often generates noncyclic flows and this means that such a technological regime is in a certain sense an unstable subsystem. However, technology has a special dependence upon an accumulating stock of information which may lead to the development of efficient compensating mechanisms (Duncan 1976).

The development of natural area protection policies and programmes has been concerned with the central theme of the preservation of the natural diversity which now exists in the biosphere (Nature Conservancy 1975). The biotic diversity is a representation of the diversity of information stored in the genetic codes of the separate organisms in the ecosystem and in the population and community structures above the individual level. The abiotic diversity is usually the result of the physical forces of the environment altering or moulding the physical elements. The development of a programme to preserve the natural diversity can be seen as a culturally developed compensating mechanism to prevent a noncyclic flow or trend.

Odum (1971) maintained that ecological succession has parallels in the developmental biology of organisms and in the development of human society. Table 2.1 gives a tabular representation of the trends to be expected in the development of ecosystems.

Table 2.1 A tabular model of ecological succession: trends to be expected in the development of ecosystems

Ecosystem attributes	Developmental stages	Mature stages
Community energetics		
1. Gross production/community respiration (P/R ratio)	Greater or less than 1	Approaches 1
2. Gross production/standing crop biomass (P/B ratio)	High	Low
3. Biomass supported/unit energy flow (B/E ratio)	Low	High
4. Net community production (yield)	High	Low
5. Food chains	Linear, predominantly grazing	Weblike, predominantly detritus
Community structure		
6. Total organic matter	Small	Large
7. Inorganic nutrients	Extrabiotic	Intrabiotic
8. Species diversity – variety component	Low	High
9. Species diversity – equitability component	Low	High
10. Biochemical diversity	Low	High
11. Stratification and spatial heterogeneity (pattern diversity)	Poorly organized	Well-organized
Life history		
12. Niche specialization	Broad	Narrow
13. Size of organism	Small	Large
14. Life cycles	Short, simple	Long, complex

	Nutrient cycling	
15. Mineral cycles	Open	Closed
16. Nutrient exchange rate, between organisms and environment	Rapid	Slow
17. Role of detritus in nutrient regeneration	Unimportant	Important
	Selection pressure	
18. Growth form	For rapid growth ('r-selection')	For feedback control ('K-selection')
19. Production	Quantity	Quality
	Overall homeostasis	
20. Internal symbiosis	Undeveloped	Developed
21. Nutrient conservation	Poor	Good
22. Stability (resistance to external perturbations)	Poor	Good
23. Entropy	High	Low
24. Information	Low	High

Source: Odum 1969

Ecological succession is defined by Odum (1971) in terms of the following three parameters:

1. It is an orderly process of community development that is reasonably directional and therefore predictable.
2. It results from modification of the physical environment by the community.
3. It culminates in a stabilized ecosystem in which maximum biomass (or high information content) and symbiotic relationships between organisms are maintained per unit of available energy flow.

The strategy of ecosystem development is similar to the evolutionary development of the biosphere, the development of individual human effort, and the development of man's technological systems – namely, increased control of the physical environment in the sense of achieving maximum protection from its perturbations. Odum (1971) makes the point that ecosystems attempt to achieve a state of equilibrium with the physical environment. In such a mature state there is found: high information content; low entropy; quality as opposed to quantity production; feedback population control; high diversity; complex life cycles and complex species interactions. Western society may be typified as being in an immature state due to:

Poor nutrient conservation
Quantity production
Linear food chains

Linear resource chains
Slowly developing feedback loops.

This situation may be changing as society starts to move towards maturity. Elements which would support this statement and agree with the mature stage characteristics of Odum's model (Table 2.1) include:

High information content
Developing feedback controls on population
High niche (professional) specialization
Complex life cycles
Complex niche interactions.

The conservation movement can be seen as attempting to move human society towards the adoption of the model of the mature state of an ecosystem. In this context, natural area planning is an attempt to develop strategies to change the existing societal trends involved in reducing the maturity of natural ecosystems (Fig. 2.1). Other conservation programmes, such as those concerned with endangered species, the conserver society and pollution control, have allied aims.

Philosophical and ideological components are developing which provide the spiritual or moralistic basis for this new approach to the environment

Figure 2.1 A mature native Scots pine (*Pinus sylvestris*) forest in central England. Ecosystems with climax biological communities are seldom encountered in most of central Europe. These woods were protected by the owner of a large estate and are now on the grounds of the headquarters of the Royal Society for the Protection of Birds.

(Passmore 1974). Dorney (1977a) has described it as an ecological triad – a reverence for life, land and diversity. Dansereau (1977) has stated that an environmentalist must collect and analyse data and must then use this data as a participant in planning. It is the function of the knowledgeable individual in society to contribute to better decisions. Those with environmental knowledge have a duty to ensure that acceptable environmental policies are promulgated.

If the past is any indication, the future philosophical and scientific bases of the environmental movement will broaden and deepen within Western society. In addition, political parties based on ecological concepts may attain a foothold in North America following the existing French and German models.

Island biogeography theory

A system of natural forested and marshy areas in agricultural and urban landscapes, each surrounded by different habitat, resembles a system of islands in a 'sea' from the point of view of species that are restricted to the islands (Fig. 2.2). Most ESAs in settled Europe, Asia and North America

Figure 2.2 Forest islands in an agricultural and urban sea.   Many natural biological communities can be visualized as islands in a sea of a man-modified communities. This is quite visible in this photograph of the agricultural development on the deep, rich soils of south-western Ontario. Historically, the farmers left 10 per cent of the land in forest for the provision of fuel and fibre. Later, small villages, such as this one named New Hamburg, grew to serve the farming community.

can be considered to be habitat islands. The theory of island biogeography deals with this phenomenon of habitat islands surrounded by a sea of altered or different habitats. This theory has developed recently and the major points in the discussion are based on: MacArthur and Wilson 1967; Diamond 1975; Moore and Hooper 1975; Pielou 1975; Diamond 1976; Diamond and May 1976; Galli, Leck and Forman 1976; Simberloff 1976; Simberloff and Abele 1976; Terborgh 1976; Whitcomb, Lynch, Opler and Robbins 1976; MacClintock, Whitcomb and Whitcomb 1977; Davis and Gleck 1978; Pickett and Thompson 1978; and Goeden 1979. The main elements of this evolving theory are summarized below.

The number of species that occur on an island is a function of the island's size and its isolation from other islands. Larger islands, and islands located close to other islands, can hold more species.

With the creation of a natural area island by the alteration of the surrounding habitat, the island initially will contain more species than it can hold at a later stage when a new level of equilibrium is established. The excess species over the new level of equilibrium will gradually become extinct. Then, the number of species in the island will depend on the interplay of extinction and colonization. The smaller the island the higher will be the extinction rate.

Each species of organism requires different minimum areas for survival. Each species of organism has a different ability to cross 'hostile' habitats surrounding the islands and therefore can require different minimum separation distances necessary to effect recolonization.

Studies which compare the number of species, S, on islands of different area, A, with similar habitats and in the same island groups have shown that the following relation is valid:

$$S = cA^z.$$

The dimensionless parameter z (the slope of regression line on a plot of the log S to the base 2 versus log A to the base 2) typically has a value in the range of 0.18 to 0.35, and c is a proportionality constant, which depends on the dimensions in which A is measured and on the taxonomic group studied (Diamond and May 1976). Given that the plot produces a series of island sizes along a straight line it is a subjective judgement on where the ideal island size is found. For example, Moore and Hooper (1975) suggested, based upon the number of bird species found in English woodlands, that nature reserves in that latitude should be 100 ha or more in size.

Given these principles, what can the designer of natural reserves do to minimize extinction rates? Figure 2.3 presents a number of geometric principles, derived from biogeographic studies, for the design of nature reserves (Diamond 1976). In general, the following design principles underlie the presented configurations.

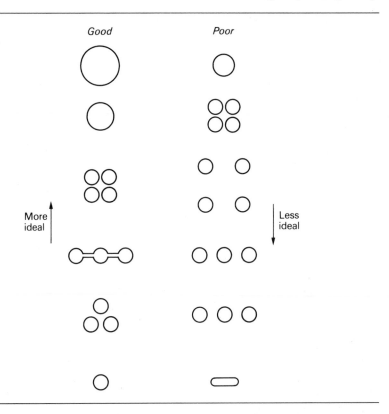

Figure 2.3 Nature reserve planning derived from general principles of island biogeography. These drawings represent the geometric shape of natural biological islands in a sea of different, or hostile, environment. In temperate climes the islands are usually forests in a matrix of agricultural or urban development. These six pairs of drawings emphasize the ideal (left column) compared to the less preferable (right column). Also, as one moves down the column less preferable situations are shown.
Source: adapted from Diamond 1976

1. A large reserve is better than a small reserve because the large reserve can hold more species at equilibrium and it has lower extinction rates. A large reserve is more capable of sustaining species higher on the food chain than is a small reserve.
2. One large reserve is better than several small reserves. If the area must be divided into a series of small reserves then they should be positioned as close to each other as possible. The close proximity of reserves will help to keep immigration rates high and hence help to ensure that recolonization takes place if local extinction occurs.
3. It is better to have a number of separate reserves positioned equidistant

from each other rather than grouped linearly. This configuration helps to maintain higher recolonization rates. In the linear configuration the end areas are relatively remote from each other, thereby reducing immigration rates.

4. The populations in reserves will be maintained at a higher level if these reserves are connected to other reserves by strips of protected habitat.
5. It is better to have a reserve circular in shape so as to minimize the dispersal distances within the reserve, and to minimize edge phenomenon. Small peninsulas of habitat may be isolated enough to have some island-like features.

These concepts are applicable to ESA designation and management. Threshold sizes, habitat linkages, area configuration and proximity are all factors which need to be considered.

Environmental planning theory

Paget (1976) maintained that the rationale for environmental planning has two main parts:

1. An overall rationale which sees the goal of planning as ecological and human development.
2. A set of criteria for guiding and judging development, namely an ecological ethic and a social ethic.

The two elements are brought together in the concept of environmental planning with the logical relations between human society (social systems) and the natural environment (ecological systems).

An ecological ethic leads to individual human acts based upon enlightenment and self-interest. It states that in the interests of all nature and in the interests of man's self-preservation, rights must be assigned to non-human nature. Limits must be placed on the actions of man. Man's responsibilities to maintain the self-renewing capability of the natural environment must be recognized.

According to Paget (1976) an ecological ethic can be stated in the following few statements:

1. Man exists in an ecological context which he can ignore only at his peril. Man is dependent upon the ecological context and the context increasingly dependent on man. The ecological context is an ecological community of organisms and environments of which man is part.
2. Man has an ethical responsibility to the community as a whole and to the individual elements of that community.
3. These responsibilities can be expressed as rights for non-human living and non-living elements in the environment.
4. Occasionally these rights may be expressed legally but in the main they exist only as ethical responsibilities of institutions such as planning.

5. An ecological ethic can be assisted by a series of principles which, derived from the behaviour of ecological systems, can guide action. These principles are enclosed with the ecosystem concept and include the concepts of resilience, carrying capacity, and protection.

Recently, Dorney and Hoffman (1979) have codified the principles mentioned in statement 5 above in order to define the environmental foci for particular planning issues, such as urban expansion, a new highway or a new airport (Table 2.2).

A social ethic deals with the principles of equity, diversity, justice, human needs and participation. According to Paget (1976) the principles of a social ethic can be stated as follows:

1. It starts from a theory of sociospatial systems focusing on the social and spatial constraints to resource accessibility.
2. A social ethic serves to protect social and cultural diversity.
3. The distributive principle aims at equal access to the resources of society and equity in the distribution of costs and benefits.
4. The redistributive principle aims at positive discrimination in favor of those disadvantaged.
5. The priority of human needs aims at determining priority needs and differentiation of needs within the population.
6. The participative principle aims at: achievement of points 2 to 5: promotion of public participation and development of democratic principles.

Therefore, environmental planning can be seen as a logical process involving the resolution of the social and ecological needs in the ordering of human actions.

Environmental management theory

Dorney (pers. comm.) has proposed that environmental management is composed of the following elements:

A. Conceptual development
    environmental research
    environmental education

B. Planning functions
    environmental planning
    environmental design
    environmental assessment
    environmental hearings

C. Site applications
    environmental monitoring
    environmental rehabilitation
    supervision of construction

Table 2.2 Technical principles of environmental management

Dorney (1977b) and Dorney and Hoffman (1979) have developed this set of
technical principles that underlie the field of environmental management. These
principles define and outline this evolving field and they are as follows:
1. Develop environmental goals and objectives
2. Evaluate new technology
3. Assess environmental impacts of new projects
4. Undertake environmental protection planning
5. Specify environmental protection measures
6. Select low risk design
7. Identify amenity/disamenity resources
8. Identify institution capability
9. Maximize flexibility or reversibility in decisions
10. Understand land-use compatibility/incompatibility
11. Community/technical/environmental information in understandable form.
12. Comply with all acts, regulations, zoning, standards and guidelines
13. Incorporate environmental quality into official plans
14. Understand historical ecosystem properties
15. Develop inventory of existing resources
16. Predict thresholds, lags, feedbacks, resiliency and limits of ecosystems
17. Identify natural processes/functions
18. Understand species population dynamics
19. Identify indicator species
20. Identify and control externalities
21. Map biological productivity of land
22. Plan for conservation/sustained yields
23. Regulate entropy
24. Identify constraints or hazardous areas
25. Identify areas serving landscape protection function
26. Identify areas offering opportunities for renovation, enhancement
27. Identify trans-boundary linkages
28. Identify unique geological/biological land units
29. Determine ecosystems stability/resiliency/diversity relationships
30. Determine carrying/assimilative capacity
31. Identify importance of land unit size
32. Identify health/nuisance landscape relations
33. Develop monitoring capability
34. Design low maintenance landscape systems
35. Understand cultural linkages between land and resources
36. Identify community values
37. Develop strategies to alter values
38. Develop educational approaches
39. Identify symbolic landscape features
40. Map recreational capability
41. Evaluate economic development strategies affecting resources
42. Encourage public participation efforts

Environmental management is intimately connected with the systems
perspective which views natural and cultural landscapes as an integrated and
interacting dynamic series of hydrological, climatological, geological, pedo-
logical, biological and cultural-technical subsystems. An environmental

manager is therefore defined as one who is involved in the provision of professional services with regard to biophysical and human ecology surveys, environmental modelling, planning, site supervision (during a building phase), biological testing of new chemicals, and monitoring present and new man-made environments (Dorney pers. comm.; Dorney and Amster 1980). An environmental planner is a person involved in one aspect of environmental management, that is planning for policy development, programme development, and land-use allocations, utilizing futures perspective and an ecological frame of reference.

Dorney and Hoffman (1979) have developed a set of technical principles that underlie the field of environmental management. These principles define and outline this evolving field (Table 2.2). ESA concerns are components of the larger field of environmental management.

There are two uses of the word management. One use has management at the end of a sequence of events that includes policy planning, data collection and inventory, plan formulation, plan approval, plan implementation and site management. In this book management is used in this context. But environmental management refers to the entire process of planning, conserving and managing the environment and its resources.

Economics

Land-use planning generally and ESA planning specifically must always deal with the situation where the costs and benefits are continually under scrutiny. Economics is a critical factor in most decisions concerning ESAs.

Economics as a body of theory deals with the allocation of scarce resources among competing demands. Economic theory has only just started to take seriously into account many of the external, ecological factors that were ignored by earlier theoretical models. Liberal market-place economics often has been criticized for its inability to deal with externalities and common property resources (Knapp 1950; Mishan 1967). Also, the assumption of economists of unlimited biospheric resources with cost, substitution and technology as the determinants is not valid.

The institution of private property ownership has evolved so that this economic system is organized and sanctioned to handle the use of things that are privately owned. Adam Smith's 'invisible hand' theory states that competition in the market-place will guide resources efficiently into uses that will produce the products that consumers want most. This model, however, applies only to resources that are privately owned and to commodities that consumers buy and use individually. If any resource is not privately owned, or if a consumer can benefit from it without having to procure and use it individually, then the invisible hand does not work.

Environmental resources which are common property tend to be used heedlessly because there are no private incentives to do otherwise (Hardin

1968; Dorfman and Dorfman 1972; Ciriacy-Wantrup and Bishop 1975). The solution can seldom be more private property ownership by individuals because it is usually not practical or even possible to exclude others from using common properties, such as air resources. There are likely to be large social-economic benefits or savings in the joint use of the resource as contrasted with individual use.

Therefore, in cases where the management of resources is to be treated as a public good the key decision is how much of these goods to provide, especially because it is difficult to restrict or stop public access to them. A social decision must be made on the degree of access to the common property.

Environmental resource management problems such as pollution, renewable resource use, land carrying capacity and non-renewable resource use are well recognized. It is obvious that there are problems, but it is not so obvious how the problems should be solved. These resource management problems cannot be eliminated – but they can be controlled. Therefore society must find the proper balance between the utility of these activities to the individual and the disutility they impose, via the environment, on others (Dorfman and Dorfman 1972).

Several writers have suggested that development must consider the carrying capacity of the environment and not only economic gain (Commoner 1971; Odum 1971; Dasmann *et al.* 1973; Hills *et al.* 1973; Miller 1975; Poore 1975). However, developing workable and defensible limits to carrying capacity is not easy. For example, the use of a renewable tree resource should not involve the destruction of the reproductive capacity of forests; but the exact number that can be taken, the allocation among various users, the timing of the removal and many other factors will require a political decision based on ecological and social, including economic, considerations.

Over time economic theorists have developed five criteria for judging ·economic performance. These five criteria are entitled:

1. The Broad Productivity Criterion
2. The Sharp Productivity Criterion: GNP ·
3. The Broad Utility Criterion: Pareto Optimality
4. The Sharp Utility Criterion: Social Welfare
5. Equity: the Distribution of Welfare

The first two criteria relate to the efficiency of the economy. The third and fourth discuss the success of the economy in promoting welfare or satisfaction. The fifth deals with the equity of distribution of costs and benefits (Dorfman and Dorfman 1972).

The Broad Productivity Criterion

An economy is said to be productivity efficient if it is producing the maximum of every good and service technically possible at the least cost to the economy, given the outputs of other goods and services and the resources used. The resolution of the use conflicts helps to produce point of optimal efficiency. For example, the production of lumber and the provision of wilderness recreation on the same piece of land may be in conflict. Many combinations of both products are possible from a given fixed input level. Obviously these two products are in conflict and therefore a balance, or a set of balances, between the two must be struck. Usually an attempt is made to seek an optimal mix versus the maximization of one to the exclusion of the other.

The Sharp Productivity Criterion: Gross National Product

In a free market the relative desirability of commodities is supposed to be reflected in their prices. Theoretically, one price unit of a commodity will provide as much consumer satisfaction as one price unit of another commodity. Therefore, if consumer demand is reflected in higher prices if the supply remains fixed the willingness to pay more implies more utility to the consumer. This suggests a social significance to prices as guides in economic activity.

The best points on a production curve are the ones at which the value of the goods and services produced is as great as possible, using market prices for the private goods and services. This suggests that the GNP, the total market value of all goods and services produced, should be as great as possible.

But the GNP criterion ignores the distribution of income. It also tends to ignore environmental impacts as well as externalities in general. Many environmental impacts take place with non-market, nonquantifiable and intangible elements. It also concentrates on short-term effects as opposed to long-term effects (Dorney pers. comm.). Many environmental features, such as many endangered species, are not marketable but they are still important components of ecosystem functioning.

The Broad Utility Criterion: Pareto Optimality

An economy ought to produce the combination of goods and services that will promote the welfare of the members of the community as far as possible within the bounds of natural and human resources and the production techniques available. The overall community welfare is some resultant of the individual welfare (utility) of each community member. The individual level of utility depends upon both his own consumption of private goods and services and the environmental conditions to which he is exposed. The operation of an economy is said to be Pareto Optimal if resources cannot be reallocated in ways that will make some member or members better off without making some other members worse off (Dorfman and Dorfman 1972).

Important social issues, such as who gets what, are raised during the consideration of various social arrangements to produce a Pareto Optimal economy. The conflicts can either be resolved by free bargaining in the market-place or by government regulation. All people use environmental resources. The welfare of individuals is partly dependent upon the quality of the environment in which they live. The destruction of sensitive environmental features for the benefit of one individual may considerably reduce the welfare of the larger community.

An economy can be productively efficient without being Pareto Optimal. Productive efficiency is a necessary condition for Pareto Optimality but it is not sufficient. Pareto Optimality is a fundamental concept and is more demanding of achievement than is the productive efficiency of an economy.

The Sharp Utility Criterion: Social Welfare

The welfare of a community is some resultant of the welfares of individual members of the community. If agreement could be reached on the method of achieving the resultant community welfare then a social-welfare function would be created. This would be a function by which evaluation of the welfare of an entire community could be calculated if individual welfares were known. The simplest function might state that the community welfare is the arithmetic sum of the individual member welfares (Dorfman and Dorfman 1972).

There are considerable problems with the definition or measurement, either in theory or in practice, of the individual utilities of community members and whether mere summation makes sense for determining social welfare. Some people use environmental features directly, for example a logger cuts and sells trees. Others use such features less directly, for example a local resident breathes oxygen produced by trees. The welfare of a community depends upon the total benefits derived from the environment by each individual. Natural ecosystems produce benefits that are of use to all members of a community, to various degrees.

Equity: the Distribution of Welfare

Equity deals with the fairness or justness of the distribution of welfare. Virtually all proposals advance some people's interests at the expense of others. In environmental decisions there is the real problem of allocating fairly the costs and benefits of environmental protection. Everyone wants to have a better environment, but few want it at their expense.

An environmental protection measure usually involves changes in the allocation of welfare: it is inherently redistributive. These redistributional effects vary greatly according to the particular circumstances of any given environmental management problem (Seneca and Taussig 1974). Any protection measure will restrict or revoke some people's long-standing practice of using the environment as they see fit, and thus reduce their welfare for the benefit of other people.

The urbanization of natural landscapes is redistributive as well. Here one intent is to redistribute welfare towards the developers and the subsequent purchasers. This is the basic reason for development activity in the private sector. In the public sector the development activity may have a distribution of welfare motive, such as a government low-income housing development.

The question of equity, the fair sharing of a society's natural environmental resources, is a key part of any environmental decision. It is also a very difficult part.

Controlling the use of the environment

The above discussion points out why ordinary economic market arrangements designed for the use of private resources usually do not lead to the efficient use of common property resources. In environmental resources that are common property, such as an airshed, a beach or a river, the various users interfere with each other. Methods are needed for allocating the use of these resources in the general interest. There are several broad classes of methods: laissez-faire; government regulation and financial inducement; and, at smaller scales, community consensus.

In the laissez-faire arrangement each potential user has free and unrestricted access to the resource. It is every man for himself. This often is, or becomes, unsatisfactory and can prove tragic for the common property (Hardin 1968).

Governmental regulation is a broad class of arrangements that can include: prohibition of certain uses, limiting of certain uses, and prescribing protective measures. All are similar in invoking the force of legal sanctions to require or prohibit specified acts that affect the resource. A financial inducement can involve the imposition of taxes or the offering of incentives for appropriate behaviour.

A basic social problem is to choose between the various types of methods of control. Various parts of this book discuss alternative environmental management arrangements developed by a number of different governments around the world for the protection of natural areas as well as for other concerns such as pollution abatement and land-use control.

The economics of natural environments

There has been an effort by a few resource economists to incorporate non-commercial, or amenity, resources of natural environments into the body of conventional resource economics. In this section we review the ideas on this subject as stated by: Fisher, Krutilla and Cicchetti 1972; Fisher, Krutilla and

Cicchetti 1974; Abrassart and McFarlane 1974; Cummings and Norton 1974; Krutilla and Fisher 1975; Bishop 1976; Kelso 1976; and Bishop 1978.

The conventional definition of what constitutes a natural resource was given by Bishop (1978, p. 11).

> Resources . . . 'become' natural resources through changes in human tastes and preferences, income levels, population levels, technologies, social institutions, and public policies. The earth's flora and fauna are part of a vast reservoir of potential resources, only a small proportion of which are recognized as actual resources at any one time.

Economic theory is based upon the allocation of human, financial and material resources to produce an array of goods and services. It is assumed that the limits to production are based upon the relevant technological development and that therefore natural resource scarcity can be overcome by technological innovation. The rising prices resulting from growing resource scarcity will force the necessary substitutions.

Many existing natural areas have alternative uses that are competitive in the free market. Among such competitive alternatives are the production of commodities that are extracted from the site, such as gravel, and can serve as inputs for further production. The natural area can also produce amenity services, such as recreational uses, that can take place on or off the site.

For the extractive commodity outputs there are well-developed economic theories as well as the market itself to provide estimates of the value of these outputs. The body of theory dealing with the production of amenity services is not as well developed.

Among the costs that must be charged against the extractive commodity value are the potential benefits lost by the act of destroying the natural area during extraction or transformation to another use. During this process the amenity services alternative may be totally and irreversibly destroyed. In the case of species extinction due to natural area destruction, it is difficult to fulfil the underlying assumptions that a rise in price of the resource, i.e. the species, will cause an increase in technological innovation that in turn could lead to an increase in supply: species cannot be recreated once exterminated. Some species can be propagated by artificial means, such as fish hatcheries, if they are amenable to captive reproduction. The other alternative to extirpation will be to find substitutes for the extinct species. Irreversibility is a key element and examples could include the destruction of a forest or the flooding of a unique canyon as well as the extinction of a species. This concept of irreversibility was attacked by Cummings and Norton (1974) who stated that there are no irreversible investment options, with the exception of species extinction. A central point here is that many environmental changes, such as the destruction of a forest, are theoretically reversible but only over a considerable length of time and possibly with considerable capital input. The destruction of a forest is reversible but only over the span of at least the couple of centuries that would be necessary for complete recolonization and regeneration to occur, assuming that suitable recolonization could take place.

The destruction of each natural area represents a possibly important reduction in the options available to society and illustrates that the expansion of choice represents a gain while the reduction of options represents a loss (Fisher, Krutilla and Cicchetti 1974). These potential benefits consist of the value of the amenities that the public would otherwise derive from the site were it left in its natural state. These benefits are compared to the benefits derived from an extractive use or a change in use. The projected stream of social benefits generated by extractive development of natural areas tends to fall absolutely or relatively over time because the resource supply ultimately is decreased to nil.

The projected stream of social benefits generated by direct, largely on-site consumption of amenity services from the same natural environment tends to rise absolutely over time due to (a) the inelastic supply of the areas (their practical nonproducibility), (b) their irreversibility in supply once destroyed by alternative development, (c) the relative (often absolute) absence of substitutes, and (d) the projected future increases in demand for such amenity services (Kelso 1976). Krutilla and Fisher (1975) point out that there is no production technology for natural environments other than natural processes.

The competing elements of the extractive versus the amenity uses of natural areas result in rising opportunity costs over time against the extractive land use. The future costs needed to reverse an extractive decision made in the present may be larger than those necessary for an amenity services decision. The consequences of a decision to allocate a natural site to a destructive development or to amenity services output may tend to weight the net benefit basis for allocative decision-making in the direction of the amenity services. Kelso (1976, p. 573) states that:

extractive commodity development of the site will impose externality costs on other (largely future) amenity service consumers of a magnitude greater than any externality costs imposed on (largely present) consumers of extractive commodities resulting from allocation of the site to the production of amenity services.

As stated earlier, environmentally based regulations are inherently redistributive. This cannot be avoided. The assessment of whether the redistribution is positive or negative depends upon the vantage point of the viewer.

The Housing and Urban Development Association of Canada (HUDAC) (1978a, b) has stated that the environmental requirements in the Region of Waterloo Official Plan create an unforeseen and costly problem for the housing industry and for the public. They felt that any environmental regulations which caused a delay in the delivery of housing units to the market caused further costs to be borne by the housing industry which would then pass them along to future buyers. They appeared to ignore any benefits that might accrue as a result of more careful planning, land allocation, site design or facility design in the housing areas. Also, the entire reduction in the options for future citizens if the natural areas were destroyed was not considered. This group was dealing with its own economic balance sheet and not with that of society.

In a comparison of two subdivisions in Waterloo, Ontario, MacNaughton (1971) established conclusions that are at considerable variance to the HUDAC view. He concluded (MacNaughton 1971, p. iii) that:

1. Single family land values were higher in the subdivision with the highest percentage of open space. The amount or quality of the open space had some degree of influence on the land values.

2. The net profits per acre appeared to be higher in the subdivision with the greatest percentage of open space and the lower number of lots per acre, or conversely there was no relationship between the number of lots per acre and the net profit per acre.

3. Amenity features such as waterbodies and natural stream channels provide a diversity of landscape and sense of space to a subdivision. This directly influences the value of abutting single family lots.

4. Because of the 'inflated' value of lots abutting an amenity feature such as a stream valley, the benefits of leaving the stream in its natural channel exceed the costs of engineering the channel to provide additional building acreage.

In 1967 the voters in Boulder, Colorado, approved a proposal to establish a fund for purchasing and managing greenbelts, financed by a 0.4 per cent city sales tax. Up to 1978 this tax had generated over one million dollars per year and over 8,000 acres (3,200 ha) of land had been purchased by the resultant programme (Correll, Lillydahl and Singell 1978). In an intensive study it was found that the presence of the open space areas had considerable impact on adjacent land values. There was a $4.20 decrease in the sale price of a residential property for every 0.3 m (1 ft) distance from the green belt. The property values adjacent to the greenbelt were 32 per cent higher than those 430 m (3,200 walking feet) away (Correll, Lillydahl and Singell 1978). The study concluded that the urban distance of a residential property from the green was related to the property's price as a quadratic curve, concave downward.

Because of the effect on the aggregate property value of the presence of greenspace, the market value assessment was approximately $5.4 million greater than it would have been without the greenbelt. This resulted in an additional $500,000 in property tax being collected each year in one of the neighbourhoods studied. The purchase price of that greenbelt had been $1.5 million, therefore the purchase price was recovered in only three years. But in Boulder the majority of the increased tax revenue, 86 per cent to be exact, went to other government bodies such as school boards rather than to the

The Little Ringed Plover (*Charadrius dubius*) has recently spread across Britain by breeding in the habitat created in flooded gravel pits. The success of this rare species has highlighted the fact that it is possible to create valuable wildlife habitat in gravel workings.

city government. Therefore the city government benefited considerably less than the above figures might suggest, but the community at large certainly benefited (Correll, Lillydahl and Singell 1978). The above study also found, while comparing neighbourhoods, that the value of open space as reflected in nearby residential property prices partially depended upon the design of the subdivision, and especially upon the walking access to the greenbelt.

It must be recognized that some of the open space referred to here is the typical park with mowed lawns, that does not fulfil any ESA criteria. Some of the open space, however, contains fine upland forests, as in MacNaughton's research area in Ontario. Are these studies of the impact of open space in general applicable to the specific case of ESAs? It is my feeling that the extrapolation from open space values to natural area values is a reasonable one. The manicured, bluegrass lawns can be converted to more natural areas by the planting and careful management of native species (Dorney 1975).

Therefore, clearly, in a number of North American situations individuals value the presence of natural landscapes in their immediate area and this is represented by their willingness to pay for access and closeness to the resource. The immediate economic benefits can accrue to both the land developer and the future home owner, but are highly dependent upon the site design.

Societal attitudes

A behaviour is dependent upon an underlying attitude. Each person uses and interacts with the natural environment in a fashion that reflects a certain

Table 2.3 Attitudes towards nature and associated characteristics

Attitude	Key indicators	Common manifestations associated with attitude	Examples of activities	Associated institutions
1. Negativistic	Common feature is the desire to avoid nature. Typical feelings are: indifference, fear, dislike, superstition, separation and alienation from wildlife	Includes a number of actions ranging from avoidance to the actual killing of animals. Animals often perceived as evil, supernatural, beyond the control of man. Very anthropocentric view. No sense of empathy or kinship with nature	Actual killing of wildlife for no particular reason. Killing to protect own life, crop or livestock. Manifestation of dislike and indifference	Land drainage subsidies. Wildlife bounties. Land clearing incentives
2. Dominionistic	Featured by a sense of superiority and a desire to master nature. Nature regarded from the perspective of providing opportunities for dominance and control. Associates with animals in order to gain a feeling of challenge, prestige, skill, superiority	Actions which display desire to control, dominate and compete with nature. Expressions of prowess and skill in competition. Considerable attachment to animals may be present	Horseback riding. Trophy hunting. Trophy fishing. Obedience training such as in circuses. Dog training. Mountain climbing	Trophy hunting clubs. Circus. Rodeo
3. Utilitarian	Nature perceived in terms of practical or profitable qualities	Animals many times perceived as an inexhaustible resource	Wildlife management, harvesting, and conservation activities	Wildlife Management Area. Camping Area in Park

	Regarded largely for its material benefits to humans Indifference to issues of animal welfare which do not affect the animal's performance or practical value Profitable qualities of wildlife are emphasized (recreation)	Nature perceived as valuable if it can be used directly for some pragmatic purpose	Hunting Fishing Commercial fish Trapping Game laws Conservation (not preservation)	Wildlife Management Department Resource Management
4. Neutralistic	A neutral view of nature Little feeling either towards or against Apathy	Disinterest Little contact with or concern for natural environment	Absence of nature-oriented activities Nature ignored	
5. Scientistic	Objective, intellectualized, somewhat circumscribed perspective of animals Animals are regarded more as physical objects for study Perceived as means for acquiring specific knowledge Emotional detachment Curiosity often constitutes the primary motivation for interest in nature	Experimentation applied on animals to acquire physiological, biological and taxonomical knowledge Animals offer opportunities for problem solving Accepts experimentations on and killing of animals for laboratory purpose Considered to be a value-free approach	Experimentation on animals for curiosity or knowledge Scientific study	Biology Department Scientists
6. Aesthetic	Associated with emotional detachment	Interest towards nature is almost exclusively on	Photography Painting	Nature Art Animal books, animal

Table 2.3 (cont.)

Attitude	Key indicators	Common manifestations associated with attitude	Examples of activities	Associated institutions
	Central interest is the beauty or symbolic properties of the animals, plants, natural environments	its artistic appeal Remains aloof from physical nature which appears to have no beauty	Sculpture Movies Viewing Animal showmanship	painting Horticulture
7. Naturalistic	Profound attraction to wildlife and outdoors Pets are seen as inferior to wildlife Wildlife as valued particularly for the opportunities it provides for activities in the natural environment Represents the 'romantic' idea of the wild Knowledge of nature is usually present	General interest in animals, specifically wildlife and wilderness Satisfaction from direct personal contact with wilderness Atavistic reward derived from experiencing wilderness as an escape from the perceived pressures and deficiencies of modern industrial life	Bird watching Wildlifers Outdoor clubs	Wilderness Areas Naturalist Clubs
8. Ecologistic	Primarily oriented towards wild and natural settings Major emphasis and affection is for species of animals in their natural setting and habitats	Marked by considerable knowledge of animals and plants Perceives man and animals as equals in a system	Study natural habitats and wildlife in wilderness Protect wildlife	Environmental Management Environmental Studies Departments

	Tends to concentrate on a systems approach including the behavioural, physical and biological components	Futuristic outlook Emphasis on preservation		
9. Humanistic	Strong personal affection for individual animals, typically pets rather than wildlife. Love felt for animals can often be compared to that felt for human beings. Philosophical and ethical principles behind empathy and concern for wildlife human centered	General concern for the well-being of all animals. Animals viewed as friends. Identification with St Francis. Plants, abiotic elements given lower emphasis than animals	Humane society Protects animals	Humane Society Pet Store
10. Moralistic	Great concern for the welfare of animals, both wild and domesticated. Has consideration for all animals and is typically more philosophical. Tendency to perceive a kinship, a sense of equality between humans and animals	Opposed to the exploitation and infliction of any harm, suffering or death of animals. Concern usually strongly held	Association of animal rights Humane Society Protects and preserves wildlife	Green Peace Movement Fund for Animals Anti hunting Organizations

Source: adapted from Bos, Brisson and Eagles 1977; Eagles 1980a; Kellert 1981

33

view of the world. The resolution of resource management issues is often based upon pre-emptory rules dependent on long-standing value concepts (attitudes and derived ideologies). An understanding of the value concepts present in a community is essential if a realistic planning strategy is to be developed.

An attitude can be described as a view of the world or a set of feelings and beliefs about an object or issue. This underlying emotional state predisposes and influences an individual's behaviour.

Kellert (1979, 1980a and b, 1981) has developed a typology of attitudes towards animals as found in American society. This classification has proved valuable as a tool to explain a wide variety of activities that take place in nature, well beyond its initial concern with animals. The typology, as modified, includes the following 10 categories: negativistic, dominionistic, utilitarian, neutralistic, scientistic, aesthetic, naturalistic, ecologistic, humanistic and moralistic. The words used for each category are descriptive of the attitude. For example, the negativistic attitude is characterized by a dislike of nature while the aesthetic is concerned with physical beauty. Each attitude is described in detail in Table 2.3.

The concepts of ecology, environmental management and natural area protection are found to the right of the scale of attitudes towards natural environments found in Figure 2.4. They are probably most closely linked with the naturalistic and ecologistic attitudes. This suggests that environmental managers may have considerable problems in justifying their approach if the attitudes of decision makers are found to the left of this scale. For example, if the county council is made up of farmers or ranchers whose attitude is largely dominionistic or utilitarian, an obvious conflict may result. Can the ecologist answer the question: what good is it? Probably he can, because the protection of natural ecosystems can be seen to be of value to all through the importance of ecosystem functioning. But, the ecologistic justification may make little sense to the dominionistic individual who sees nature as a means of establishing personal dominance or individual accomplishment. The moralistic view, with its constituent closely felt emotional state may be viewed as being too 'emotional' by those with the scientistic attitude who see themselves as being value-free and objective.

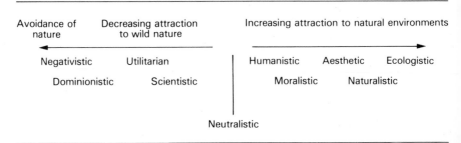

Figure 2.4 A scale of attitudes towards natural environments

This range of attitudes towards nature is found throughout W/ society. Factors such as geographic location, cultural background, tu. education and socioeconomic status appear to be important progenitors of attitude groupings in society.

In a democratic society it is essential that the environmental manager understand the underlying attitudes of both the public and the key actors. Such an understanding will facilitate the development of policies, plans and management strategies that may have a better chance of implementation.

Summary

Many necessary components of the biosphere are not part of the market economy. Many common property resources, such as air, water and genetic diversity, are necessary for ecosystem functioning and therefore for human life. Traditional economics is not capable, in itself, of acting as the sole basis for resource allocation or for determining the use of all environmental features.

Research into the fields of ecological theory, island biogeography and the institutional arrangements surrounding environmental management has produced a basis of theory that is conceptually advanced. Models of ecosystem functioning are now capable of predicting future impacts of human action. Therefore, anticipatory planning is both feasible and defensible.

The protection of Environmentally Sensitive Areas by municipal governments is one necessary component of a general societal environmental management strategy. These local natural ecosystems when considered as a unit are important as genetic reserves, contribute to the supply of useful products, serve as benchmarks for areas of intensive utilization and help maintain essential ecological processes.

CHAPTER 3

Designing a planning and management strategy

Introduction

Planning is future-oriented. It is aimed at conscious intervention at a time in the future, based upon past and present conditions (Paget 1976). Planning for environmental purposes involves a knowledge of ecological processes as well as the societal decision-making processes that determine resource use. An organizational framework governing the investigation of ESAs should consist of four basic components (Nelson 1978) that include:

1. Ecology.
2. Technology.
3. Perceptions, attitudes and values.
4. Strategies and institutional arrangements.

This provides the broad investigative structure which was generally followed in the research for this book.

Ecology was discussed in Chapter 2. A consideration of technology involves an understanding of the processes and functions dealing with production of material objects. Technology and its associated economics have had considerable impact on the natural functioning of most ecosystems (Fig. 3.1). The limitation of technologically induced stresses on the ecosystem is a major component of both pollution control (after the fact) and environmental impact assessment and prediction (before the impact).

The perceptions, attitudes and values of the citizens of a society influence their behaviours. If nature is valued it will be protected. If it is disliked it will be abused. Under a democratic form of government it is essential that the planner understand the attitudes of the public with whom he deals. This is especially the case at the municipal level where public opinion is made known quickly and effectively to the authorities.

Similarly, the attitudes of the decision makers themselves, the elected officials and the resource managers are key elements. Resource managers

Figure 3.1 Gravel extraction eating away at a remnant woodlot. Surface mining involves the complete removal of the surface terrestrial ecosystem. This woodlot is a remnant of the forest that covered this land in south-western Ontario before clearance for agriculture.

with a single resource focus or a commercial-use bias may be antagonistic to a strategy that emphasizes ecological diversity. The general public in many countries in northern Europe and North America are often more sympathetic to a broadly-based protection philosophy than are many resource managers who see their job as utilizing the resources to fulfil a specific industrial function or economic demand.

Nelson (1978, p. 48) states that:

> Institutional arrangements refer to forms of government, agencies, civil and criminal laws, legislation, and other means of influencing human behaviour and effects on land use. The term includes what has been referred to as social guides: rules and regulations, penalties and other enforcement, performance standards, subsidies, taxes, and other means of inhibiting or encouraging change. Also, to be recognized as institutional arrangements are social phenomena which often have an indirect and unappreciated effect on land use and landscape.

Municipalities are the local governments that manage the cities, towns and villages. They usually obtain funds from a tax on the land within their borders. Grants from senior levels of government are obtained for both operational and capital expenditures. Local governments often have jurisdiction over the development and use of land. As a result they are important determinants of landscape quality and urban form.

Each municipal government is unique. Its responsibilities have been defined by many years of interaction with senior governments. It has a populace with a particular set of values. It has expertise in its employees and officials. Over the years it has developed a certain approach to making the decisions that are necessary. A specific issue, such as the need for environmental management, must be carefully integrated into the existing government structure. The institutional arrangements which are critically important for the design of an ESA planning and management strategy include: the existing policies and programmes: the public participation structures now in place: the economic data available; the legal setting and the planning expertise of the municipality.

The development of an overall strategy for the planning and management of ESAs requires a knowledge of the various institutional structures and arrangements that have a bearing on decision making. A plan is only as good as its implementation. A plan is implemented only when it is feasible and acceptable.

Programme arrangements

The overall goal is to manage land use so that significant natural areas are passed on to the future with their ecological features and processes unimpaired (Fig. 3.2). Any programme that attempts to fulfil this goal must be carefully designed if implementation is to occur (Kusler 1980).

Municipalities have two basic options for natural area conservation. They can arrange purchase by themselves or by another government and then manage the land as they see fit. Or they can influence the use of the land by the owners or inhabitants. This latter option is the one discussed in this section. From the perspective of a municipal government a large number of institutional arrangements should be considered during programme planning. The most important of these are discussed in three general categories: ecology, law and politics.

Ecological considerations

1. Long-term resource protection and management must be given priority over short-term economic gain.
2. An environmental data bank is necessary. An ESA programme requires that data be accurate and acceptable to the various users. Due to time and cost restrictions, collect necessary data but avoid the trap of collecting all the information it would be nice to have. Cooperative arrangements with a local college or university can be very valuable.

Figure 3.2 Road construction through urban wetland.   This sensitive wetland forest in Kitchener, Ontario was given official ESA status after regional road networks had already been planned and partly developed. Roads stopped at both sides of the swamp at the time of Official Plan designation and it was too late to reroute or halt their linkage. Anticipatory, county-wide inventories and policies help to solve such conflicts before they arise.

3. The collection of data on the ecological features is best done by a shared public and government arrangement. The use of local expertise, if available, can produce a cost-efficient documentation. In addition, local rapport and sympathy with the programme is developed.
4. The use of standardized definitional criteria is advisable. The definitions should be clear and understandable. This assists political acceptability, ensures consistency across municipalities and reduces cost.
5. The ESAs must be defined by boundary lines on maps of either 1:50,000 or 1:25,000 scale in rural areas; 1:10,000 may be more useful in urban areas. Boundaries should correlate with visible ground features. Environmentally sensitive areas tend to be relatively permanent landscape features. Further precision can be obtained by detailed field surveys once a land-use change is proposed.
6. In-depth studies may be necessary in those areas that are subject to development threats in the near future. Anticipatory actions are preferable to reactive actions.
7. Environmental impact assessments can provide data that are useful for detailed boundary delineation, comparison of alternatives, assessment of long-term consequences and development of management plans. The cost of data collection should rest with the developer.
8. Buffers may be necessary. They cannot be designed until the proposed activity is known and its impacts assessed.

Legal considerations

1. The programme must be legally acceptable within the framework established by the governing legislation.
2. A balance must be struck between the land development rights of the landowner and the ecological common property rights of the public.
3. It is necessary to shift proposed incompatible uses out of ESAs.
4. The use of performance standards for land-use regulation is preferable to outright activity prohibition. The amount of restriction should not be greater than necessary. Make an attempt to allow private economic land use while limiting negative environmental impact.
5. Attempt to integrate ESA programmes with other resource management efforts such as hazard lands, water basin, open space, recreation and forestry concerns.
6. It is often politically necessary to concentrate on new developments only, thereby eliminating the possibility of creating legal noncomforming uses or stopping existing uses.
7. Consider structural developments (buildings, roads, services), nonstructural developments (landfills, surface grading, open pit mines) and site productivity alterations (agricultural clearing, intensive forestry, biocide usage).

This bumblebee (*Bombus humilis*) has declined throughout central England due to the habitat loss associated with the clearing of forests and hedgerows for the intensification of agriculture. Since 1945 large amounts of natural wildlife habitat have been destroyed in lowland Britain.

8. Regulations should be applied fairly and equally in private as well as government activities.
9. Ensure that all local policy plans (Official Plans, Structure Plans, Master Plans) contain broadly-based resource management policies as well as specific ESA policies.
10. Ensure that the implementing zoning by laws and ordinances are put in place so as to implement the policy plan.

Political considerations

1. It is usually easier to build an ESA programme within the existing government regulatory structure than it is to develop an entirely new agency.
2. Political acceptability is necessary with four major groups: local politicians, municipal staff (engineering, planning, parks and recreation are particularly important), the development industry, and the general public.
3. It will be necessary to have a environmental planner on staff for both policy development and plan implementation. Flexibility and imagination are necessary personality attributes.
4. Adequate programme funding is necessary. This may be shared between governments.
5. Information dissemination is an important feature. Agencies and individuals cannot fully assist with site management if documentation is

41

lacking. Publish the ESA maps and supporting data so that all interested and involved parties can be aware of the areas and their features.

6. All interested government agencies (federal, provincial, state, soil conservation board, conservation authority, water authority) involved in various aspects of resource management should be kept informed of the programme. Direct participation by these agencies in programme design and operation is desirable.

7. A policy of encouraging public involvement throughout the planning process can help produce politically acceptable policies and reduce public distrust.

8. Sympathetic members of the public are often prepared to assist with many facets of the programme including important elements such as data collection, boundary delineation, policy development and public education.

9. Adjacent municipalities should be encouraged to develop similar programmes. This will ensure consistency across municipal boundaries and will reduce the possibility of developers using the divide-and-conquer technique to obtain approval.

10. Long-term plan enforcement, monitoring and site management is necessary. This can be shared among a variety of governmental levels with the involvement of interested members of the public.

11. Environmental education programmes in schools, parks and in the mass media can assist in fostering a public awareness of the need to conserve ESAs.

Summary

A number of ecological, legal and political considerations must be taken into account in the design of an ESA planning and management strategy. Any plan must be legally, politically and financially acceptable or it cannot be implemented. It is possible to integrate ESA protection policies into the existing municipal government decision-making structure.

Key elements of an ESA planning and management strategy include:
The integration of ESA conservation into the existing structure
The development of environmental data base
The development of a municipal staff expertise in environmental planning
The use of environmental education to foster public awareness.

CHAPTER 4

Planning guidelines

Introduction

Environmental planning represents an attempt to integrate ecological concerns into societal decision making. For the last few decades it has been an add-on to the existing blocks of knowledge deemed to be important. It came after the economic, social and societal power-group factors were considered. Environmental planning is now attempting to become premeditative. The protection of natural areas is considerably facilitated if preparatory inventory, delineation and management work has been done before land-use developments are proposed.

Environmental planning represents an attempt to strike a balance between ecological capability and societal desirability. Some development in a natural area may be highly rated by certain segments of society but the development may be ecologically undesirable. Several writers have suggested that development must have regard for the carrying capacity of the environment as well as for economic gain (Commoner 1971; Odum 1971; Dasmann *et al*. 1973; Hills *et al*. 1973; Miller 1975; Poore 1975).

Methodology

This chapter outlines a standard methodology for ESA planning. The methods are based upon the experience that planners have obtained in this field.

The case studies discussed in Chapter 6 come from Great Britain, Japan, Canada and the United States. Each political jurisdiction must develop its own set of institutional arrangements but certain planning principles are applicable in a wide variety of situations. The treatment in this chapter contains elements common to the examples presented in Chapter 6.

Programme differentiation by scale

Natural area programmes take place at a variety of levels of government organization (national, provincial, regional, municipal and private). To provide a method for the resolution of potential conflicts and jurisdictional overlap between the levels, it might be worth while to consider the idea that each level concerns itself with a different scale of activity.

Sullivan and Shaffer (1975) proposed that a country requires a system of nature reserves that vary in size and number in an inverse relationship. The largest reserve, of 25,000 sq. km, would provide suitable habitat for stable populations of the largest predators. They then proposed two reserves of 12,500 sq. km and so on until thousands of small reserves under 300 ha in size would be required for the system. Canada and the United States have a rough equivalent of such a system now, with the ESAs starting to fulfil the need for the inclusion of many small areas.

Table 4.1 outlines a seven-level hierarchy of land units that vary in scale from 1:8,000,000 at the largest to 1:5,000 at the smallest (Udvardy 1975; Brady *et al.* 1979). In this hierarchy, the national level of concern would be on natural areas of national significance within the realm and biome land units scales. The realm is a biogeographic unit of continental size, for example the nearctic realm in the northern hemisphere. The biome is a slightly smaller unit that contains entire biotic regions, such as the North American prairies. These very large classification units can provide a basis for national government system plans. The provincial or state concern

Table 4.1 A proposed system of programme and land-unit scales for Canada

Land unit description	Approximate scale	Map units	Government level	Normal size of area of concern
Nearctic realm	1:8,000,000–1:30,000,000	one unit	federal	above 1500 ha
Biome	1:3,000,000	four units	federal	
Land region	1:1,000,000–1:3,000,000	500–1500 ha	provincial-state	1500 ha to 400 ha
Land district	1:500,000–1:1,000,000	160–400 ha	provincial-state	
Land system	1:75,000–1:450,000	80–150 ha	municipal	less than 400 ha
Land type	1:50,000–1:20,000	5–75 ha	municipal	
Land subtype	1:5,000	1–4 ha	municipal	

Source: adapted from Brady *et al.* 1979

would be on natural areas of provincial or state significance within the land region and land district unit scales. Finally, the various municipal governments would concentrate on natural areas at the land system, land type and land subtype unit scales.

The ESA concept applies equally well to the case of significant natural areas in large expanses of relatively natural ecosystems, such as occur in large parks, as it does to remnant natural areas in the agricultural and urban landscapes of developed areas. That is to say, within very large parks there could be discrete areas that fulfil one or more ESA criteria.

It is important to recognize that this evolving practice of municipal involvement in natural area planning and management is part of larger nature conservation initiative that ultimately involves all governmental levels.

Criteria of identification and classification

The words Environmentally Sensitive Area comprise an official title conferred on any area that is designated in an approved plan. Such an area is recognized as containing an ecosystem whose biological and physical integrity and ecological processes should be protected and maintained. In a very few cases, sites have been designated because of geological or physiographical features only, but normally designation is primarily based upon the biological characteristics.

The most successful criteria developed so far have appeared independently in Canada and in Great Britain. Since the theoretical ecological basis is similar it is not surprising that the criteria are similar.

The national inventory of biological sites of importance in Great Britain used a standard set of criteria for assessment and site selection (Ratcliffe 1977). The key words of each criterion and a brief description of its use are given below:

1. Size – the importance of a site increases with the geographical area which it serves.
2. Diversity – higher numbers of species and of communities is desirable.
3. Naturalness – a natural community is one that is unmodified by human activities.
4. Rarity – the protection of rare or local species is an important consideration.
5. Fragility – different communities have different degrees of sensitivity to environmental change. Priority should be given to those that are least able to withstand alteration.
6. Typicalness – it is important to include representatives sites within a conservation system plan. These typical or commonplace communities may be widespread in distribution.

45

7. Recorded history – those communities with long histories of scientific research are important because of the opportunity to document long-term trends.

8. Position in an ecological/geographical unit – the ability of a site to represent a large number of the characteristic ecosystems of a geographical area is important.

9. Potential value – some sites are at present in an altered state but have the potential to illustrate appropriate management, reclamation or successional changes.

10. Intrinsic appeal – some sites have an intrinsic appeal due to widespread community interest or the presence of important groups such as birds.

The inventories undertaken in the Province of Ontario in Canada have used a standard set of criteria for selection of those sites considered as Environmentally Sensitive Areas. The criteria were developed over time and have been precisely worded and defined (Eagles 1980b).

1. The area represents a distinctive and unusual landform within the municipality, Ontario or Canada.

2. The ecological function of the area is vital to the healthy maintenance of a natural system beyond its boundaries, such as, serving as a water storage or recharge area, important wildlife migratory stopover or concentration point, or a linkage of suitable habitat between natural biological communities.

3. The plant and/or animal communities of the area are identified as unusual or of high quality locally within the municipality, Ontario or Canada.

4. The area is an unusual habitat with limited representation in the municipality, Ontario or Canada, or a small remnant of particular habitats which have virtually disappeared within the municipality.

5. The area has an unusually high diversity of biological communities and associated plants and animals due to a variety of geomorphological features, soils, water, sunlight and associated vegetation and micro-climatic effects.

6. The area provides habitats for rare or endangered indigenous species that are endangered regionally, provincially or nationally.

7. The area is large, potentially affording a habitat for species that require extensive blocks of suitable habitat.

8. The location of the area, combined with its natural features, make it particularly suitable for scientific research and conservation education purposes.

9. The combination of landforms and habitats is identified as having high aesthetic value in the context of the surrounding landscape and any alteration would significantly lower its amenity value.

These criteria evolved independently from those used to delineate national and local Natural Reserves and Sites of Special Scientific Interest in Britain. However, in both cases an attempt has been made to represent the important features and functions of an ecosystem that can be measured and are adaptable to the practice of land-use planning.

In practice, these criteria may result in the selection of atypical areas as opposed to representative areas. For example, emphasis is often placed on late successional stage communities. Thus, in their application, consideration must be given to the representation of each major community type in the overall system.

The absence of such criteria considerably weakens any planning effort to protect natural areas. The criteria fulfil the following functions:

1. They allow a relatively systematic comparison of different sites. The degree of fulfilment of one criterion or the number of criteria fulfilled can be used to rank different sites.
2. They help to outline the importance of the sites to decision makers. A careful reading of the criteria gives one a basic understanding of what the policy initiative is concerned with.
3. They help direct research efforts towards the further definition of certain concepts, i.e. considerable research on the definition of rarity has been stimulated.
4. They help to ensure similar approaches in municipalities that are separated geographically.
5. They help in the process of drawing boundaries, as only those features that fulfil the criteria are included.

No standardized criteria are used for the definition of ESAs in the United States. In practice these words have been applied to hazard lands (floodplains, organic soils, unstable geology), wetlands (swamps, marshes, estuary, salt marshes), recreation areas (parks, reserves), biological areas (forests, prairies, coastal zones), scenic areas (waterfalls, valleys) and historical features (battlefields, forts, habitations) (Thurow *et al.* 1975; Kusler 1980). The Montgomery County General Plan (1969) presented criteria for those unique natural areas that should be given priority for park and open space acquisition which included:

1. Scenic vistas
2. Areas which should remain in a natural agricultural or developed state due to soil conditions, flooding, etc.
3. Areas possessing unique natural features in topography, woodland and rock outcroppings
4. Significant surface water areas, floodplains, wetlands and aquifer recharge areas
5. Cultural and historical buildings and sites.

This mixture of cultural and environmental features can make policy development and site management difficult. Dorney (1977a) suggested that it is preferable to divide the environment into three subsystems for environmental assessment purposes: cultural-historic, abiotic and biotic. This is the *de facto* approach used in Canada and Britain. This book is concerned with the biotic areas and makes a clear distinction between these and the areas of cultural significance and the hazard lands.

Interdisciplinary team studies

A team of knowledgeable individuals with disciplinary qualifications is needed to study, identify and recommend ESAs using the criteria. The team approach is a critical element. No one person has the experience, technical knowledge or skill to apply all the details of the criteria. Well-functioning interdisciplinary teams can produce solid plans that tend to be more capable of withstanding the assaults of critics.

In most cases information from the following subject areas will be involved in the research, delineation and planning: pedology, hydrology, climatology, geomorphology, ornithology, herpetology, ichthyology, mammalogy, botany, zoology, ecology, history, environmental planning and management.

Research teams have been sponsored by a wide variety of government and private bodies. Some of these have included:

An independent research team assembled and sponsored by a national government nature conservation agency

A group of university students working under the direction of a senior professor and sponsored by a research grant

The members of a consulting firm sponsored by local municipal government

The staff of a resource management agency.

No matter what institutional environment surrounds the research team, similar field technique, data collection, data analysis and report compilation methods can be utilized. The interdisciplinary approach is important. Consideration of all major facets of the environment requires a substantial knowledge base.

The inventory process

Natural areas are remnant landscapes which have not been converted to intensive urban, commercial or agricultural uses. Some of these primeval areas contain bogs, swamps, woodlots, marshes, floodplains, lakes, natural and man-made landscapes. The aim of an inventory is to identify their location and some of the ecological dynamics of such ecosystems. A regional perspective must be maintained in order that decisions can be made concerning the criteria that ask for a decision on the regional status of a species or phenomenon. The resource inventories are compiled to outline the regional environment and to find areas in that environment which fulfil one or more of the criteria.

The physical environment

A detailed resource inventory of the regional and local physiographic features, landforms and bedrock materials including the groundwater and soils is undertaken. In most of settled North America and Europe this information is available on topographic maps, soils maps and geology maps. Most of these are at a 1:50,000 scale. The overall climate of the region is an important ecological factor. Areas with significantly variant microclimates may harbour unique ecosystems and rare species. Invariably, however, such communities are found through vegetation inventories rather than through climatic inventories.

Hydrology deals with the role and behaviour of water as it circulates through the system: ocean-atmosphere-land-biosphere. Human activities often affect the hydrological cycle as well as the water quality of surface and subsurface reservoirs. Initially, it is necessary to inventory the location of surface reservoirs, groundwater aquifers and groundwater recharge areas. The interrelationships between these units must be considered.

The hydrological regime is usually of immediate importance to the residents. Water in appropriate quality and quantity is necessary for ecological, agricultural, residential, commercial and industrial uses. Therefore areas which play particularly vital roles in the hydrological regime are important to the community at large.

Areas of high water-table and good water quality should be located. In the South Wellington study in Ontario (Eagles *et al.* 1976) areas of high water-table were defined as those areas with soils where water remains at or within 30 cm of the surface for 8 to 10 months of the year. Water quality data of surface water bodies are usually available from the government environment agencies.

Groundwater recharge areas allow sufficient water to percolate downwards into the soil and ground for replenishment of the groundwater. Where rainfall is abundant and proper soil conditions exist, upper level acquifers are recharged. Well-drained soils which are developed on materials with high infiltration rates, such as sands and gravels, have little surface runoff. Those which have sufficient overburden over the underlying bedrock to retain adequate amounts of groundwater are considered as potential groundwater recharge areas (Eagles *et al.* 1976). In some areas the overall regional hydrological regime has been investigated so that critical decisions could be made regarding the role of individual natural areas within the regional environment.

Such close study on parent materials, soils and groundwater will reveal

49

the potential quality and quantity of available groundwater. The possible contamination from agriculture, animal feedlots, surface disposal wastes, septic tanks, mine drainage, pesticides and other chemicals must always be considered. The impact of construction in areas upstream from an ESA may cause water problems in the natural area. The effects of water-caused erosion and the distribution of snow are two other factors that might be considered.

The biological environment

A detailed resource inventory of the biological communities and their component populations of birds, mammals, reptiles, amphibians, fish, plants, and sometimes insects is undertaken to establish regional occurrences and population levels.

The research team must make judgements on the relative frequency of occurrence of each species within the region, province or nation. Some of these species will turn out to be rare and therefore possibly in danger of extirpation. Desmond and Vessey-Fitz (1974) observed that plants are rare because of restricted range, because they are not well-known species, or because of direct destruction of the plant or its habitat. Such rare species may be saved by investigating the dynamic status of their community, ascertaining the effects of change on their survival, and limiting negative change. Transplanting and propagation can be considered as alternatives but usually are expensive and are impossible for many rare species.

The biogeography of the flora and fauna is important information for decision-making. Where they exist, regional studies examining the status of individual species within a geographically delimited area are helpful for the determination of rarity or uniqueness. Generally, regional-level botanical inventories are not available in the United States and Canada but are in Great Britain.

A list of all species found within the ESA is made. All communities are mapped. Are the species common, uncommon, rare or endangered? Are there new species that had not been discovered or recorded previously within the region, province or country? How do the biological communities within the study area fulfil the criteria such as: an unusual habitat with limited representation in the region, province or nation; an area with a high diversity of biological communities; and a habitat for rare species? The research team can gain insight into the natural history of local areas by consulting local citizens, naturalists, government personnel and groups who have such knowledge.

All activities in and adjacent to the ESA that may affect its ecological values should be identified. Such activities could include excavation and earthmoving, dredging and landfill, draining, dumping, waste disposal, burning, erosion, logging, vegetation cutting, economic and residential activities, industrial and commercial structures, litter and old vehicles, urbanizátion, pollution, and extensive use by recreational and all-terrain vehicles. The data needs are summarized in Table 4.2.

Table 4.2 Summary of data needs

Factor	Comments
Existing biological data	1. Published inventories 2. Private field notes and memory 3. Government unpublished inventories 4. Data banks: atlas inventories, nest record schemes, herbaria.
Existing physical data	1. Soil, geology maps 2. Hazard land and floodplain mapping 3. Hydrology surveys 4. Data banks: well logs, exploration drill records.
Data scale	1. Based on existing topographic maps 2. 1:50,000 or 1:25,000 in rural areas 3. 1:10,000 in urban areas.
Inventory-offsite	1. Aerial photographs – as recent as possible and as old as possible for comparison 2. Satellite imagery for large areas.
Inventory-onsite	1. Interdisciplinary team 2. Field inventory of each community type 3. Detailed field notes, photographs.
Data analysis	1. Comparison to region-wide surveys 2. Placement of information into data banks (files, herbaria, specimen collections) 3. Screening for significant features.
Display format	1. Maps (boundaries delineated) 2. Reports (data dissemination) 3. Files (permanent storage) 4. Photographs.

Interpretation and application of criteria

The identification, description, classification and analysis of each landscape unit for the existence of significant natural values must be accomplished. The following is a summary of the interpretations of each of the Canadian criteria listed earlier.

Canadian Criterion 1 (distinctive and unusual landform)

The distinctive and unusual landforms are usually defined by earth scientists. There are usually significant geological phenomena that illustrate specific land evolution processes or landforms. Examples could include glacial artefacts such as kames, eskers or old beach levels.

Canadian Criterion 2 (vital ecological function)

Detailed analysis of soil structure, depth and type as well as bedrock structure, well-log information and published groundwater information allows the hydrologist to delineate the importance of a particular area with respect to its hydrologic functions. Important wildlife migration stopover points can be considered. The biological linkage of habitats by a section of unbroken similar habitat is essential for the movement of individuals and species. Island biogeography has shown that the number of species in a natural area will be maintained at a higher level if the natural area is connected to another such area by a strip of similar habitat.

Canadian Criteria 3 and 4 (high quality communities)

The existing knowledge of the past conditions of various habitats and communities along with the current review of knowledge of habitat and community distribution in the county allows decisions to be made concerning the diversity and amount of each habitat and each community. Knowledge of conditions before European settlement in North America can be particularly valuable but is seldom available (Chanasyk 1970). On particularly ideal sites high quality communities may develop. Such communities may represent conditions that are not widespread. Therefore, to preserve all of the ecological diversity of a county, such communities are worthy of protection. Unusual communities may be the result of a number of ecological or cultural factors. They are not widespread, by definition, and add a component to the overall diversity of the county.

Canadian Criterion 5 (high diversity)

The overall ecological stability (the resistance to external perturbations) of a county and of a community type is enhanced by maximum diversity. Diversity can be represented by the information found in species, populations and communities. A high diversity of biological communities in an area is determined using aerial photography, published information and field surveys. Records of a high diversity of flora and fauna from many types of communities indicates a high community diversity. An area with high diver-

Figure 4.1 Yellow Mandarin (*Disporum lanuginosum*) is a rare plant according to the *Atlas of the Rare Vascular Plants of Ontario*. This plant has a distribution which brings it into the extreme southern portion of the Province of Ontario. It is therefore nationally rare in Canada, provincially rare in Ontario and regionally rare in the few counties in which it still exists. It occurs in two stations in Halton Region (Sutherland 1981). Atlases such as this are invaluable for the determination of species distribution, abundance and therefore conservation importance. Environmental planners can concentrate their effort on the location and habitat of rare species.
Source: *Atlas of the Rare Vascular Plants of Ontario* (Argus and White, 1982)

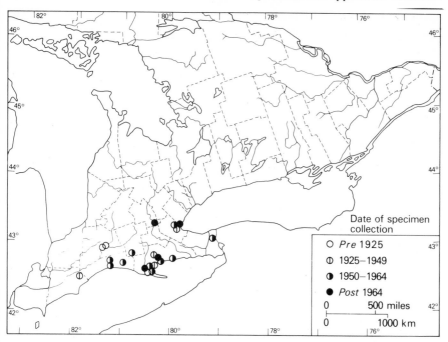

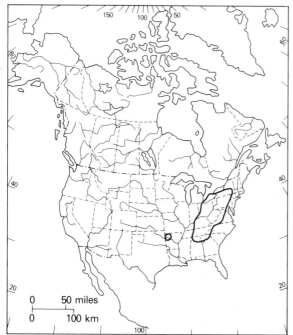

HABITAT: Rich beech-maple-hemlock woods on brown forest soils and dry, sandy woods.

STATUS: Rare in Canada and Arkansas.

Date of specimen collection

○ *Pre* 1925

◐ 1925–1949

◑ 1950–1964

● *Post* 1964

0   500 miles

0   1000 km

53

sity would be one with many community types present (aquatic, marsh, lowland, upland) or a wide range of species within one community type, or both.

Canadian Criterion 6 (Rare species)

This criterion discusses three levels of species rarity: regional, provincial and national.

At the regional level it is necessary to have region-wide biogeographical data before the individual status of one species can be ascertained. To standardize the use of this criterion a number of conventions have come into general use. If any species of a relatively easy-to-identify and well-known group, such as plants, mammals or breeding birds, occurs at 10 stations or less in a region it is considered to be rare. For other groups, such as the herpetofauna, fish or invertebrates, a level of five stations or less is used. The latter groups are handled in this way to avoid the magnification of a rarity which is due to insufficient data. A station is defined as a community that is mappable at a 1:50,000 scale.

At the provincial, state or national levels it is usually necessary to resort to published references concerning individual groups. The development of atlases of the flora and fauna has proved very useful for the determination of species distribution and frequency of occurrence (Figure 4.1).

Canadian Criterion 7 (large area)

Island biogeographical theory states that a large reserve is better than a small reserve because the large reserve can hold more species at equilibrium and has lower extinction rates. Upper level predators, such as bobcat (*Lynx rufus*) and Cooper's Hawk (*Accipiter cooperii*) require extensive blocks of habitat for long-term maintenance of stable populations. Typically, areas larger than 400 hectares (1,000 acres), with a high proportion of undisturbed natural landscape, fulfil the large and undisturbed category. However, these sizes are not sufficient for bear, cougar or wolverine.

Canadian Criterion 8 (scientific research, conservation education)

Significant natural resources combined with facilities and ready access for educational uses are needed in an area before it is deemed suitable for educational purposes. Scientific research is a broad subject and potentially could encompass almost any ESA. Up to now this criterion has only been used in the case of long-term and recognized scientific studies that are now taking place. In the future, ESAs could prove to be valuable sites for research into many elements of the island biogeography and ecology theories discussed earlier.

This criterion has been questioned because it outlines specific uses, such as scientific research and conservation education, while other uses such as hunting, birding or photography were excluded. Nevertheless, most counties have felt that scientific research and conservation education are important enough general-use categories and are sufficiently intimately connected with the ecological/physical characteristics of the ESA to be recognized as valid reasons for the definition of an ESA.

On another level, many public bodies, such as Conservation Authorities, that have a role to play in ESA conservation find it important to be able to discuss the more immediate use of an ESA for research and environmental education along with its long-term ecological importance to society. Environmental education is necessary for the development of a community understanding of the importance of ESAs.

Canadian Criterion 9 (aesthetics)

High aesthetic value usually relates to: high topographic variability; natural communities forming a backdrop or skyline with an urban context; or individual site components such as waterfalls, high vantage points and cliffs.

This criterion does not directly deal with the biological/physical characteristics of the ESA but with these characteristics as represented in aesthetic appeal. The aesthetics are a way of measuring an area in terms of visual appeal as opposed to number of species or degree of rarity.

From my experience this criterion is one that is most easily understood and accepted by the general public. However, it should not be used alone. It is best applied if an area fulfils at least one of the other criteria.

The following is a summary of the interpretations of each of the British criteria listed earlier.

British Criterion 1 (large size)

In a heavily utilized landscape such as that of Great Britain those semi-natural communities that remain tend to be isolated and small. The lowland forests are often islands in an agricultural sea while the upland moors and heaths are often larger but are on isolated ridges and peaks. The largest sites are capable of supporting species with larger area requirements, such as those of higher trophic levels, e.g. Red Kite (*Milvus milvus*). The larger the site the more value it has for environmental conservation.

British Criterion 2 (diversity)

Sites with large numbers of species and communities are preferred. It is especially important to represent ranges of variation, as might occur with altitudinal zonation or successional level. Since it is not possible to compile a comprehensive inventory of all species of communities, emphasis is often placed on well-known groups such as birds or herbaceous plants. Species richness is a relative factor in that it is comparable to another similar ecosystem elsewhere.

British Criterion 3 (naturalness)

The attempt here is to find those ecosystems with the least amount of human-caused alteration. In a highly developed area such as England very little of the landscape has completely escaped some modification. This situation is common across Northern Europe and Japan and is fundamentally different from North America where considerable amounts of pristine landscape still occur. The abundance and dominance of introduced species is one measure of naturalness. Given the slow dispersal rate of most plants compared to animals, the degree of naturalness is more important to botanists than to zoologists. Since most areas are disturbed to some degree, the occurrence of pristine areas in northern Europe is of considerable scientific importance. Change cannot be measured without having a benchmark.

British Criterion 4 (rarity)

In Great Britain, rarity for individual species tends to be defined on three levels: international, national and within the four constituent 'states' (England, Scotland, Wales and Northern Ireland). Of these levels, particular importance is given to the protection of species that are rare within the nation of Great Britain. Emphasis has been placed upon the vascular plants, lichens, bryophytes, birds, mammals and two insect groups, Lepidoptera and Odonata, because of the available distributional knowledge.

The development of large numbers of atlases has assisted the systematic determination of species distribution and frequency of occurrence. For example, rare British vascular plants are defined as being those that occur in 15 or fewer of the thousands of 10 km grid squares in Great Britain. The *Atlas of the British Flora* was the first of its kind in 1962. Since that time breeding birds (Fig. 4.2), mammals, reptiles, amphibians, bumblebees, butterflies, dragonflies and other groups have been inventoried within the national British grid. These atlases are invaluable data bases that are the envy of others in countries which lack such information. Information on the various atlases and the ongoing research projects can be obtained from the Biological Records Centre, Huntingdon, Cambridgeshire, England.

The rarity of some species is closely tied to the rarity of the associated habitat. Those small areas that contain rare species in rare habitats can be considered automatically to be sensitive to disturbance because of the relative amount of loss that could occur.

British Criterion 5 (fragility)

This criterion deals with the sensitivity of communities, species and associated

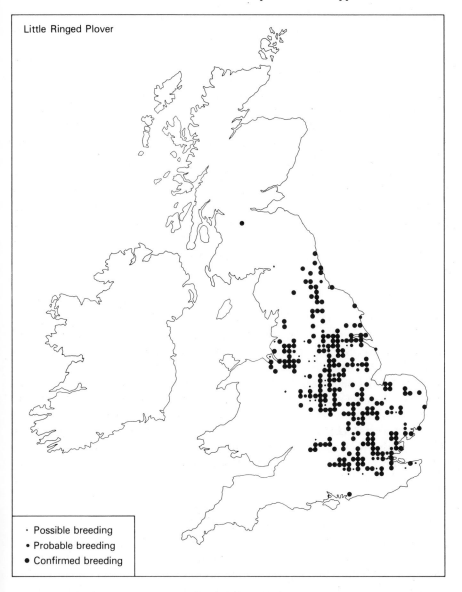

Figure 4.2 Atlas map of the breeding locations of the Little Ringed Plover (*Charadrius dubius*) in Great Britain. The species moved into the British Isles using gravel pits as its primary breeding habitat. Country or state/province-wide inventories such as this are quite helpful in determining the status of any particular species. Those in small numbers should be given conservation priority. *Source*: Sharrock 1976

habitats to environmental change. Some ecosystems, such as those in early successional stages, are inherently prone to natural change and may require management intervention if a certain state is desired. Most ecosystems are sensitive to man-induced change but some are less able to survive activities such as recreation or resource exploitation. Fragile sites are often uncommon fragments of previously widespread ecosystem types. Their rarity is closely tied to their inability to survive alteration.

British Criterion 6 (typicalness)

It is important to represent the typical and widespread features in a nature reserve system. This criterion tends to help balance the influence of the other criteria that screen for atypical or unique sites. This type of ecosystem can be of particular importance in providing a benchmark or baseline for scientific research. Typical, average sites may exist near to or within others that can be considered to be unique because of rare species or unusual physical features.

British Criterion 7 (recorded history)

The presence of data from long-standing scientific research can add to the value of a site. Such a situation will make a site more valuable than another which is equivalent biologically but lacks such information. For example, paleobotanical data from acid wetlands can illustrate the evolutional history and give a good idea of the long-term processes shaping the environment.

This criterion is subservient to those that describe the existing ecological value of a site. This criterion is difficult to apply in the sense that any site can be used for some form of scientific research and that when research is started on many sites the relative historical research value of any one site is gradually reduced.

British Criterion 8 (position in an ecological/geographical unit)

It is important to protect a site that includes in a single geographical area many different ecosystem types. Therefore, two habitats in close proximity are more valuable from a conservation point of view than are similar habitats widely separated. The theories of island biogeography point out that contiguous habitats can protect a higher species diversity than separated habitats. From a management standpoint, there is a practical advantage in having different key sites close together.

British Criterion 9 (potential value)

Certain ecosystems have the potential of developing far greater nature conservation value over time than exists at present. Examples could include heavy logged woods, excavated peatlands or some gravel workings. This value may develop naturally or may be encouraged by active management intervention. It is useful if such potential sites are near to other sites with high nature value.

British Criterion 10 (intrinsic appeal)

Some species or groups of organisms have higher profiles in the eye of the general public. Therefore, they have a resultant higher political profile. Similarily, science has not treated all species equally. Some groups are well known while others are poorly known. A good deal of emphasis is placed on birds, on their breeding areas and on areas of migration significance.

A comparison of the British and Canadian criteria is found in Table 4.3. The criteria are similar in the two countries.

Table 4.3 Comparison of British and Canadian criteria

Criterion	Britain	Canada	Comments
Distinctive landform		X	Not directly considered in Britain
Vital ecological function		X	Included in other criteria in Britain
High quality community	X	X	Naturalness in Britain
High diversity	X	X	Similar in both countries
Rare species	X	X	Similar in both countries
Large area	X	X	Similar in both countries
Scientific research	X	X	Similar in both countries
Aesthetic		X	Not directly considered in Britain
Fragility	X		Fulfilment of other criteria considered to indicate fragility in Canada
Typicalness	X		Canadian sites may be atypical
Position in a unit	X		Similar to vital ecological function criteria in Canada
Potential value	X		Not considered in Canada
Intrinsic appeal	X		Not a separate criterion in Canada but considered in other criteria

The use of the criterion in a country is shown by an X

Boundary delineation and adjustment

Boundary delineation involves the detailed interpretation of site-specific resource data. The boundaries should contain the characteristics which fulfil the criteria. With the help of air photo interpretation and intensive field studies, biological and physical communities within the areas are identified. The boundaries of the environmental area enclose the biological communities which merge into one another through transition zones. The boundaries are usually delineated, based on an abrupt change in habitat resulting from present and past land use. Some of the boundaries may correspond to soil type changes. Others may be vegetation community boundaries such as forest edges or the water/land interfaces. The presence of the boundary does not suggest a complete break in biological and physical interaction. For example, many areas provide habitat for several rare and uncommon species of plants and birds, contain a high diversity of communities and serve the vital ecological function of groundwater recharge and storage. These ecological functions are tied to landscapes outside the defined site.

Boundary delineation is one of the most difficult decisions facing the environmental planner. It involves the careful consideration of biological, landscape, ecological and political factors. The most important factors to be taken into account are:

The visibility of the biological community boundaries

The potential impact of and on adjacent land uses

The territory or home range of rare or otherwise critically important species

The natural boundaries of changing environmental features such as tides, flood lines, erosion areas, and depositional areas

The nutrient/matter inputs to the area from upstream or upwind resources

The ecological integrity of communities that are close together but not in direct contact. In such cases linkages should be considered

The number or diversity of community types that are desirable for long-term protection

The recent or proposed land developments in the area

The alternative uses of the area.

The role of advisory committees

A number of government jurisdictions have established advisory committees to provide advice on ecological matters. They are primarily technical in nature in that they provide comments from an ecological perspective on a wide variety of development, planning and management issues. Those that are the most productive and politically acceptable attempt to represent a broad range of environmental expertise in their membership. For example, it is desirable to have knowledge of the following disciplines represented: zoology, botany, aquatic biology, forestry, wildlife management, environmental law, civil and chemical engineering, landscape architecture, regional geography, environmental planning, resource conservation, town planning and outdoor recreation. In specific cases additional specialities may be required. The important point is that the committee members represent their

The endangered Japanese Crane (*Grus japonensis*) has a total world population of approximately 400 individuals. About 200 cranes are in a non-migratory group in south-eastern Hokkaido. They spend their summers in marshes and their winters in open water streams. Even though individual cranes are given protection in Japan their marshland breeding habitat has been partially destroyed in the last two decades. High breeding levels are necessary because approximately 10 per cent of this Japanese population is killed annually by collision with power lines near the feeding areas. The conservation of any wildlife species must start with the protection of critical breeding habitat.

disciplinary knowledge, not the organization they work for or are connected with. The members must act as independent citizens of the community and it must be made clear that their actions do not reflect the official position of their employer. If this is done correctly the committee is more likely to attract experienced and capable individuals who are willing to volunteer their time and energies to community benefit. The members usually serve without remuneration except for out-of-pocket expenses.

The committees usually report to elected councils or council committees. With this arrangement their advice goes directly to the decision makers. At the same time the council realizes that it has the final authority and no feelings of infringement of authority should result (Fig. 4.3).

These committees are examples of both an interdisciplinary team approach and the role that private citizens can play in advising elected officials. It might be illustrative to briefly outline the experience of one such advisory committee. The Regional Municipality of Halton in Ontario, Canada is a restructured County that has the authority for region-wide planning. The provincial government established a number of Regional Municipalities in the late 1960s and early 1970s to provide a local government unit capable of handling the problems of the rapid urban growth occuring in the heavily populated industrial and commercial area of southern Ontario. An Ecological and Environmental Advisory Committee (EEAC) was estab-

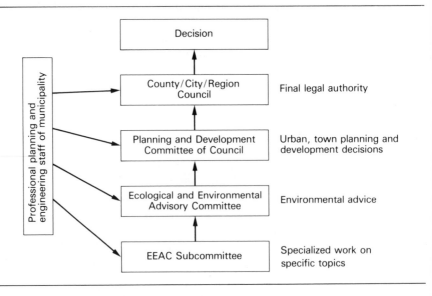

Figure 4.3 Reporting role of advisory committees

lished in 1976 by the Regional Council which is the body of elected aldermen or town councillors. The Advisory Committee reports to the Planning Committee which is composed of elected politicians and is a subcommittee of the Regional Council.

In the Region of Halton the EEAC has dealt with a variety of environmental issues that have direct relevance in the municipality. Examples have included the establishment of a new sanitary landfill, the location and construction of oil and gas pipelines, the forest management policy of the Provincial government, the control of leachate from old landfills, and many urban design and development projects. The emphasis has been on land-use problems and the protection of Environmentally Sensitive Areas. The committee had a large role to play in the development of the environmental policies of the Regional Official Policies Plan.

The terms of reference of the Halton Ecological and Environmental Advisory Committee, as adopted by Regional Council, are given below.

1. To asist the Regional Government and the Regional Planning Department in the development of an Official Plan for the Regional Municipality of Halton which would be in keeping with the area's desire for a high quality, natural environment.
2. To recommend (to the Regional Planning Committee) studies to be conducted in areas where any development might have an impact on the

environment and to review, comment and undertake studies based upon information contained in development reports.

3. To examine issues of a natural, ecological or cultural nature referred to the committee by various levels of government, Committee members, public and private groups, and individuals.
4. To be aware of studies being conducted by various levels of government and regulations being drafted and to comment on them with respect to their impact on the environment of this Region.
5. To examine issues which would affect the natural environment of the Region and to make the Committee's opinions known to the appropriate regional Department head and Committee.
6. To encourage, undertake or commission studies that will lead to a better understanding and enhancement of the Region's environment.
7. To undertake an educational programme explaining the nature of the Committee, the environmental goals of the Region, and the ways individuals and groups could assist in the attainment of these goals.
8. To serve as a coordinating agency for representatives of diverse regional viewpoints on environmental issues.
9. To extract and interpret, from the data available, areas which have a potential high social value for the management of such features as:
   (a) unique cultural features
   (b) water quality
   (c) unique natural features
   (d) wildlife
   (e) groundwater recharge
   (f) forested areas
   (g) agriculture
10. To provide an input into the formulation of terms of reference for Regional and senior governmental studies of significance to the Regional environment.

The committee appears to be a well-accepted and respected institution with this local government. Its advice has been carefully thought through and is generally considered to be conservative. Some elected officials have stated their pleasure at being able to get broadly based advice on issues that can be complex and difficult to handle.

Advisory committees lose their effectiveness if they start to assume that they are the decision makers. The elected officials soon point out who is in power and the resultant conflict often serves to reduce the influence of the committee's advice.

Advisory committees, such as the one just described, are in use in municipal governments in many countries. In the case studies discussed in Chapter 6 such committees were found to be in place in Japan and Great Britain as well as in Canada.

Application to municipal plans and governments

The primary thrust of the effort described in this book is the protection of natural areas by local or municipal levels of government. The inventory information, however, is useful to agencies of provincial, state and national government in their planning deliberations.

After the identification of Environmentally Sensitive Areas within a municipality, the next step involves the development of appropriate planning policies and guidelines which will assist in the protection of the areas. A preferred municipal treatment is for the areas to be protected by the tool of the official policies plan as constituted under the relevant legislation. In addition, rural and urban valleylands and wetlands can often be protected under special purpose valleylands of floodway policies.

A set of recommended policies for Environmentally Sensitive Areas are given below.

1. As a general rule, no development is permitted in sensitive areas due to the detrimental impact.
2. Certain public works may be carried out, subject to environmental impact analysis, provided that intrusion can be made without detrimental environmental impact and that no other feasible alternative is available.
3. A sensitive zone does not imply that areas will be purchased by a public agency or that areas are open for public use.
4. Land-use designation and controls are to be specified in the by-laws and regulations implementing regional and local official plans.
5. Municipal by-laws should encourage and permit the municipality and/or other agencies to undertake management agreements with the owners of sensitive areas.
6. The boundaries of sensitive areas shown on maps in regional and local official plans should be accepted on the understanding that more precise boundaries may be established as required through an environmental impact analysis.
7. If lands designated as environmentally sensitive are proved to be endangered by a proposed nearby change in land use, means of protection should be available to, and be considered by, the municipal council.
8. Addition of other lands to those designated, or deletion of areas which have been degraded, may be carried out by amendment to the official policies plan upon recommendation of persons or agencies, provided that detailed studies justify such action.
9. The alteration of any condition or land use of a sensitive area which may affect the natural values for which that area was designated must be approved by the appropriate authority, based on site plans and management plans submitted by the owner of the sensitive area.
10 Procedures for applications for alterations in conditions or use are to be prepared by the municipality. These procedures should also include

specific requirements for conducting environmental impact analyses.

11. Agreements for management of designated areas may include financial cost sharing, adjustment of property assessment, rebates of property tax, definition of rights and responsibilities, provisions for public access, specific natural resource improvements, or any other provision deemed necessary to ensure continuance of the sensitive area.

12. There should be provision for minimum setbacks from any sensitive area, sufficient to ensure its preservation.

13. Sensitive areas should appear as a land-use designation in official policy plans and zoning by-laws, and not as an overriding development control over a variety of land-use designations.

14. Appropriate enforcement procedures and staff must be set up to ensure effective implementation, enforcement, supervision of any official policies plan, management plan, zoning by-law, or other regulation.

The legal and political realities of each individual municipal jurisdiction will dictate the amount of emphasis to be placed on the adoption of the policies. The set given above attempts to introduce ESAs in the municipal decision-making framework and give them a profile that dictates their consideration during any discussion of land-use alteration. The policies do not deal at all well with agricultural or forestry development because of their traditional isolation from normal municipal planning. This issue has been discussed in Great Britain because of the large-scale negative impacts of intensive farming and commercial forestry (Watkins pers. comm.) Provincial, state or national governments, depending upon the country, usually have farming and forestry policies with associated administrative agencies. The municipal authorities must be prepared to enter into discussions with such agencies if a comprehensive ESA policy initiative is to be implemented.

Planning summary

The resource inventory and analysis process is within the larger context of resource management and urban and regional planning. The environmental data must be able to complement and compete with the economic, social and political forces that shape plan formulation and approval.

The planning context may exhibit considerable variance from municipality to municipality. The detailed planning structure and implementation strategies will therefore have to be developed independently each time.

Nevertheless, certain common elements are present in each plan. These have been discussed in this chapter. A simplified planning summary is given below. It is expected that appropriate public involvement will take place at each significant decision stage of the planning flow.

1. Goal formulation

2. Regional (County) study
   (a) Identify natural assets of the region by literature research.
   (b) Carry out field survey studies in the region. Collect data on both physical and biological resources. Present data in both tabular and map form.
   (c) Document historical ecology and human history of the region.
3. Local areas study
   (a) Identify, catalogue and map natural assets of the individual areas. Select areas that deserve protection and management in the light of the selection criteria.
   (b) Document functions and values of the natural areas: ecological, cultural, economic and aesthetic.
4. Written report on the location and features of all ESAs in the region.
5. Written policy recommendations at the county or regional level of government.
6. Incorporation and designation of natural areas in official policies plan – drafting and review. Council approval.
7. Application to the upper government level for final approval.
8. Upper government approval and official designation.
9. Plan implementation.
10. Site management.
11. Site and system monitoring

The site monitoring and plan administration functions are critical to the long-term success of the programme: a plan is only as good as its implementation. Normally, municipal governments have planning departments with professional staff to handle the issues. The long-term site monitoring is almost never done by municipalities and must be undertaken by other agencies or private groups. The use of environmental advisory committees helps to solve many of these needs. The committee can be a constant watchdog for problems. Its members may be able to either undertake the site monitoring themselves or to arrange for it to be done. The development of monitoring and administration of the programme is essential.

CHAPTER 5

Site management guidelines

Introduction

Management can be seen to be at the end of the following sequence of events: policy planning, data collection and inventory, plan formulation, plan approval, plan implementation, site management and monitoring.

The purpose of site management of an ESA should be to ensure the long-term maintenance of the features for which the site was designated. Intensive manipulation may be necessary but in most cases the preferred method would be to let nature run its course. Probably the most frequent management activity will be to guard against negative influences that could harm the features of the site.

This chapter discusses the management of existing ESA's. A detailed case study will be discussed in order to give an example of the circumstances and problems that may arise.

Site management plans

The management of an Environmentally Sensitive Area is a complex and never-ending process of monitoring and assessing the activities that surround and impinge upon the area. Various upper-level government agencies, such as the national and state/provincial park organizations, have experience in the management of natural sites but this capability is usually lacking in municipal governments.

Site management requires knowledge of the dynamics of the ecosystem in question as well as an organizational structure for carrying out long-term management. Each of these needs will be discussed in turn.

What should be the purpose of the site management? This is the first question to be asked. In the majority of cases management of ESAs will be concerned with maintaining a natural ecological community with minimal disturbance by man. Since climax ecosystems essentially maintain themselves, managers must watch for influences which limit natural renewal or reduce the successional level.

Management may involve the protection of specific species, such as those on the edge of their range or those that are endangered. Natural processes may need to be altered to maintain a species' habitat. For example, the US Fish and Wildlife Service undertakes habitat manipulation and predator control in its programme of reintroducing the endangered Whooping Crane (*Grus americana*) to the continental US. This previously extirpated species has been introduced to a protected wetland ecosystem, Grey Lake National Wildlife Refuge in Idaho, in an effort to increase population numbers (Anonymous 1977a,b, 1978a). The ecosystem is actively manipulated for the purpose of single species management. Such management must be carefully considered because taken to extremes it can result in diversity reduction. Very few natural areas in urban areas will contain anything as exotic as a Whooping Crane, but the concept of single species management may still have to be considered carefully. The manipulation of an ecosystem for the production of one of a few particular species is philosophically divergent from management to ensure maximum ecological diversity.

Natural disturbance may be critical to maintaining ecosystem diversity. Recognition of this fact may be difficult both conceptually and practically. Fire is an important environmental determinant in prairie and grassland ecosystems. The ecological role of fire is becoming well recognized in North American prairies and active burning regimes are implemented. For example, the native prairies owned by the Nature Conservancy in Minnesota are burned to retard woody growth and to stimulate the native herbs. Invading non-native grasses usually are susceptible to properly timed fires while native grasses are better adapted (Searle and Heitlinger 1980). In Ontario, portions of an excellent long grass prairie near Windsor have been purchased by the city and the provincial government (Pratt 1979). The open growth is slowly being closed in by woody growth. Fire is badly needed but the area is surrounded primarily by residential development and so political and safety concerns have so far limited any management burn from taking place. But small fires are frequently started by local children and these have accomplished some of the much needed burning. This is one of the rare cases where vandalism is fulfilling a management objective.

Certain species of wildlife can cause considerable landscape alteration. The American beaver (*Castor canadensis*) cuts trees and constructs impressive dams and ponds. This self-created habitat is important for predator avoidance, winter survival, food collection and food storage. But what should be done if beavers start to flood a unique bottomland plant community? Should the animal be removed to protect the botanical variety? The answer may be determined on the relative status of these two features within the country environment. If beavers are widespread but the botanical

Table 5.1 Components of a site management plan

1. Determination of management objectives
Protection of ecological diversity
Population increase of endangered species
Increase in habitat diversity
Retardation of ecological succession
Water level manipulation
Commercial product extraction

2. Biophysical inventory of ESA and adjacent lands
Soil mapping/geological features
Slope determination
Surface hydrology characteristics
Biological community mapping
Plant and animal inventory in each community

3. Human impact determination
Inventory of human uses and disturbances
Frequency and duration of uses
Key actors
Grazing
Logging
Surface mining
Garbage dumping
Utility corridors (hydro, gas, oil, water lines)
Residential/commercial/industrial construction
Outdoor recreation use
Water or air pollution

4. Management priorities for each community
Level of alteration allowed or encouraged
Preferable amount of resource extraction allowable
Methods for reducing harmful uses
Manipulative methods (burning, cutting, damming)
Protective methods (fences, wardens, education)

5. Human actor/institution inventory
Land ownership
Local environmental attitudes
Government agencies with similar objectives that could be of assistance
(State/Provincial Parks, National Parks, Soil Conservation Boards, Conservation
Authorities, Water Boards, Parks Commissions)
Private organizations with similar objectives that might assist (Horticultural
Society, Nature Conservancy, Heritage Groups, Naturalist Clubs, Hunt Clubs,
Historical Associations, Sierra Club, rural estate home owners)
Organizations that might oppose environmental management (developers,
Chamber of Commerce, forestry companies, local industry)

6. Development of suitable institutional arrangements
Work with sympathetic landowners
Be careful to not alienate neutral groups
Develop appropriate mix of encouragement/education/agreement/lease/contract

Table 5.2 Site management possibilities

Ownership	Management group	Form of agreement
Municipality (fee simple)	Municipal Parks Department	Employer–employee
Municipality (lease)	Municipal Parks Department	Employer–employee
Municipality (fee simple)	Nation/Province/State – forestry	Forest management agreement
Municipality	Nation/Province/State – fish and wildlife	Fish and wildlife agreement
Municipality	Nation/Province/State – endangered species	Endangered species habitat management contract
Municipality	Cons. Authority/Board	Management contract
Municipality	Consultant	Contract
Conservation Authority/Water Board/Soil Conservation Board	Nation/Province/State – forestry	Forest management agreement
Conservation Authority/Water Board/Soil Conservation Board	Nation/Province/State – fish and wildlife	Fish and wildlife agreement
Conservation Authority/Water Board/Soil Conservation Board	Nation/Province/State – endangered species	Endangered species habitat management contract
Conservation Authority/Water Board/Soil Conservation Board	Consultant	Contract
Conservation Authority/Water Board/Soil Conservation Board	Cons. Authority	Employer–employee
Club (Naturalist, Horticulture)	Club	Volunteer
Club	Cons. Authority	Contract
Club	Consultant	Contract
Church	Committee	Volunteer
Corporation (non-profit)	Consultant	Contract
Private individual	Municipality	Agreement

Table 5.2 (cont.)

Ownership	Management group	Form of agreement ·
Private individual	Nation/Province/State – forestry	Forest management agreement
Private individual	Nation/Province/State – fish and wildlife	Fish and wildlife agreement
Private individual	Nation/Province/State – endangered species	Endangered species habitat management contract
Private individual	Cons. Authority	Contract
Private individual	Consultant	Contract
Private individual	Private individual	Handshake, verbal or none

community is the only one of its type then probably the beavers should be removed.

The presence of certain features, such as a large tree blown down or poisonous plants, may create a public nuisance to adjacent property owners. These might have to be dealt with quickly and without detailed knowledge of the effects of the events or the management response. However, if anticipatory biophysical inventories have been done then some information will be available to help with decision making.

The more resource information is available, the better the opportunity for skilled ecosystem management. The ultimate goal should be the production of a detailed management plan for each ESA (Table 5.1). This plan would be based on biophysical inventories carried out in the field.

Poore and Gryn-Ambroes (1980) suggested that a management plan should fulfil three requirements. First, the plan must be based on a comprehensive analysis of the conditions of the site. Second, specific resource policies should be stated so that individual land uses can be assessed within an objective framework. Third, the plan is more likely to be implemented if the affected community is involved in the plan development. Landowners, interested scientists, naturalists, outdoor recreationalists and environmental educators may desire to participate.

Assuming that site management priorities have been identified, there are many possibilities for the job of implementing the plan. Table 5.2 gives an extensive list of possibilities and illustrates that institutional arrangements for site management are really only limited by the creativity of the manager.

In the vast majority of sites the government or sympathetic private groups will not purchase the land. The natural ecosystems will stay in private ownership. For protective purposes no arrangement can surpass that of ownership by a sympathetic and knowledgeable landowner. The owner can take pride in the features he owns and thereby provide excellent and continuous monitoring and protection. In three detailed case studies of ESAs in Ontario it was found that sympathetic landowners occurred in each area (Brobst and Eagles 1977; Ralph and Eagles 1977; Tobias and Eagles 1977). The good quality natural ecological conditions were recognized and appreciated by a majority of the landowners. These studies indicated that at least in Ontario the condition of many of the remnant ecosystems is partly the result of careful landowner management. The existence of these ESAs was not solely the result of historical land clearance patterns and benign neglect. Such a situation is ideal and must be carefully considered. Many landowners are willing to take care of their land but they do not want some government agency to tell them that they have to do it. Clumsy and insensitive approaches may harm a potentially valuable situation.

Hoose (1981) outlines many examples of cooperative landowner agreements for natural area management in the United States. He discusses the hard-earned knowledge of the Nature Conservancy in delineating and protecting important natural areas. A variety of methods for dealing with landowners is discussed.

Not all landowners will be sympathetic or interested: if a municipality sees the need to implement a management plan it may have to purchase the land. The money for purchase may be shared with other interested levels of government. For example, in many areas the state or provincial forest management agencies have funds for commercial forest purchase and management. Similar arrangements may be available for nature reserve, fish and wildlife or endangered species purposes.

Special purpose agencies such as Conservation Boards or Water Boards exist with resource management mandates that are at least partly compatible with natural area conservation. Their objectives might be dovetailed with those of the ESA planner. Some compromise may be necessary and possible from both approaches.

The mobilization of local human resources should be given priority. Landowners are more willing to listen to people they know. The basic encouragement of pride in and concern for one's community can often be extended to the local woodlot or wetland.

If a municipality could mobilize the human resources of a community the job of site management would be more easily facilitated and cost reduced, as has been shown in Austria. In that country nature wardens are appointed by the local governmental authorities and have the following responsibilities (Fossel 1973):

To explain to the general public the basic ecological principles and man's role, especially his responsibility within the environment

To protect the environment and survey tourist facilities such as shelter cabins, footpaths and picnic spots

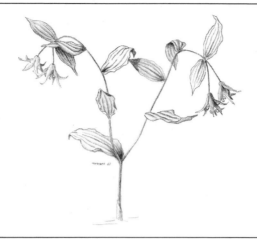

Yellow Mandarin (*Disporum languginosum*) is found from southern Ontario through to Alabama and Georgia. In Canada, at the northern edge of its range, it is rare and found only in rich, mature woods. Those populations that have survived this extensive forest clearance are in need of conservation protection. The species is both provincially and regionally rare and therefore fulfils the associated ESA criterion discussing rare species. Extreme southern Ontario contains many species of plants and wildlife that are restricted within Canada to this area of moderate climate.

To ensure that laws, rules and regulations are obeyed and to prevent their violation by timely appearances, warnings or legal steps against persons who have committed a punishable act.

In Austria there are now 7,200 nature wardens acting in a voluntary and honorary capacity (Fossel 1973). This approach is also used in British National Parks. It was widespread in Ontario in the last century for game management but was abandoned with the development of paid, professional game wardens.

The impact of the local advisory committees discussed in Chapter 4 is an excellent example of the energy and knowledge that can be mobilized on a volunteer basis from the community. This same principle could be used to develop a group of volunteers who would help in all aspects of planning as well as management of ESAs.

A site management plan case study

The development of a management plan for a natural area designated for protection by the municipality but remaining in private ownership is a novel concept. To explore the possibilities and constraints, three different areas were chosen for study in Ontario, Canada during 1977. One was an upland complex of native deciduous forests with scattered conifer plantations and old fields (Ralph and Eagles 1977). One was a lowland mixed swamp forest along a high-quality trout stream (Brobst and Eagles 1977). The other was an old field-alvar complex with scattered native deciduous forests and conifer plantations (Tobias and Eagles 1977). The three major ecosystem types (upland forest, swamp, alvar) were chosen to explore the management needs of different biological communities.

To illustrate the approach and findings, one case study will be summarized. The Beverly Sparrow Field/Hyde and Rockton Forestry Tracts are located on a limestone plain in the Regional Municipality of Hamilton-Wentworth. The Region is immediately west of the Halton Region to be discussed in Chapter 6. The two forestry tracts are owned by the Regional Government (formerly Wentworth County) while the prominent alvars are privately owned. The alvars are open, short grass fields that have developed in thin soil over a limestone bedrock. The forestry areas came into county ownership due to tax default during the depression years of the 1930s. The areas, which were farms then, were reforested with a variety of conifer trees according to a forestry agreement with the Provincial Department of Lands and Forests, now the Ministry of Natural Resources. Since then this provincial agency has managed the lands for forest production purposes.

The Hyde Tract is 142 ha in size; the Rockton Tract, 131 ha. The open field alvar is owned by several landowners with the Klaas Christmas Tree Farm holding the vast majority of the 130 ha. In total the area is 508 ha.

The area was recommended for designation as an ESA by a consultant in 1976 (*Ecologistics* 1976). It was included in the Regional Official Plan passed by Regional Council on 17 June 1980 and approved by the Province of Ontario on 26 June 1980.

To develop a management plan a number of site inventory and mapping projects were undertaken. A short history of the site was prepared. Landscape dynamics are better understood when one can correlate visible features with known historical events and dates. This is particularly important for developing an estimation of ecological succession rates and dynamics. At the same time a land ownership map was compiled. This was necessary for contacting the landowners for permission to enter their property. Physical factors such as climate, surficial geology, soils, and hydrogeology were mapped according to existing data sources and aerial photographs. Relatively comprehensive biological inventories were undertaken with specific research categories being vegetation, amphibians, reptiles, birds and mammals. Species lists, site locations and numbers of individuals were compiled. All of this was published in a report and made available to all landowners and relevant government bodies (Tobias and Eagles 1977).

Figure 5.1 shows the vegetation communities of the area. The most frequent plant associations are: old field, upland deciduous forest and conifer plantation. Smaller areas of sedge meadow, marsh, lowland decidous forest

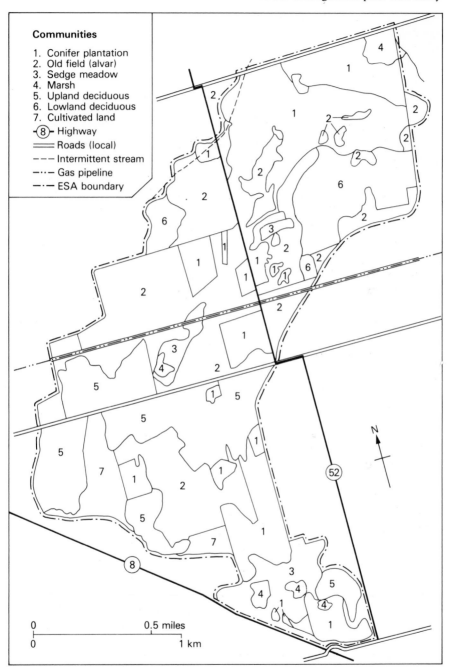

Communities

1. Conifer plantation
2. Old field (alvar)
3. Sedge meadow
4. Marsh
5. Upland deciduous
6. Lowland deciduous
7. Cultivated land
-⑧- Highway
═══ Roads (local)
− − − Intermittent stream
−··− Gas pipeline
−·− ESA boundary

Figure 5.1 Beverly Sparrow Field, Hyde Tract and Rockton Tract vegetation communities. The development of a management plan requires a basic inventory of the ESA. Vegetation communities are indicators of land use as well as microsite conditions. Wildlife populations are in turn influenced by the habitat created by plants.
Source: Tobias and Eagles 1977

75

Figure 5.2 Beverly Sparrow Field alvar community. This short grass community has developed on thin soil over a bedrock of limestone. Individual shrubs and trees are slowly invading the fields from nearby woods. The development of management strategies for an early succession stage community requires consideration of active techniques to retard succession.

and cultivated land also exist. The entire area has a thin soil underlain by limestone bedrock. This situation has been described by some as an alvar (Fig. 5.2) (Catling *et al.* 1975). Much former farmland is now a mixture of natural shrubby regrowth and conifer plantations. Some open alvar has been planted with conifers as a commercial Christmas tree farm. These trees are allowed to grow to 2 metres in height and are then cut and sold. A continual rotation cycle has been established so that some areas have small trees while others are nearing harvest.

The site is best known for its significant breeding bird community. Tobias and Eagles (1977) documented that 21 of the 81 recorded breeding species in the ESA are uncommon in the Hamilton-Wentworth Region. Thirteen of these species were on the 1977 Blue List which is a list of species that are undergoing noncyclical population declines in North America (Arbib 1976).

Apart from the presence of rare species, the avian community of the Beverly Sparrow Field, as the alvar is known to local naturalists, is unique in two respects: composition and diversity. The seven species having the highest population densities during the breeding season were found to be six species of sparrow (Field Sparrow, Song Sparrow, Savannah Sparrow, Grass-hopper Sparrow, Chipping Sparrow, Clay-coloured Sparrow) and the closely related American Goldfinch. No other known communities anywhere in Ontario exhibit a similar compositional structure (Eagles 1976). Overall the Sparrow Field contained 38 breeding species (Eagles and Tobias 1978). This is exceptionally high. All the breeding bird surveys conducted in Ontario from 1955 to 1975 in similar habitat (fields with trees) were compared by Eagles (1976). He found the average number of breeding species in this type of habitat was 14.5 ± 3.2 (95% confidence) while Tramer (1969) in an analysis of all eastern North American surveys found a similar figure of 14.08 ± 2.31 (95% confidence). When these two figures are contrasted to the diversity of the Sparrow Field (38 species), it can be seen that the alvar supports a unique breeding bird population. When the breeding habitat of the other biological communities is added the high bird species diversity becomes noteworthy.

The 1976 report states that the site fulfils several of the ESA criteria outlined in Chapter 4: numbers 3 (high quality plant and/or animal communities), 5 (high diversity), 6 (rare or endangered indigenous species), and 9 (aesthetic value). Subsequent research suggests that it also fulfils criteria 7 (large in size) and 4 (unusual habitat with limited representation) (Tobias and Eagles 1977).

At present there are only a few factors negatively impacting on the site. These factors include the construction of a few single, family homes and the presence of a gas pipeline. Another gas pipeline was installed in 1975 and the disturbed area is now becoming revegetated.

The two forestry tracts are owned by the Hamilton-Wentworth Region and managed by the Ministry of Natural Resources according to a forest management agreement. This management has taken the form of reforestation by various species of conifers. The long-term aim is to establish the conifers as a nurse crop for a future deciduous forest. Over the next 30 years the conifers will gradually be thinned and then removed as the deciduous trees seed in naturally and begin to grow.

No large-scale activities that will affect the ESA in a negative fashion in the foreseeable future are planned. Only small-scale agricultural changes are anticipated.

After the site inventories were completed a meeting was held in the informal atmosphere of the principal researcher's home. All landowners and representatives of relevant government bodies were invited. Draft recommendations were presented by the researchers and discussed. The point was stressed that the exercise was privately initiated and that the landowners were under no obligation to agree with the study conclusions.

Management recommendations

The principal management objective should be to preserve the present land uses and corresponding high biological diversity. This entails maintaining the existing diversity of vegetative community types. All landowners and managers, private and government, could carry on much as they had in the past. This objective can be achieved if the current management policy of the privately-owned Christmas tree plantation is continued and the current long-term Regional and Provincial Government's management policy for the publicly-owned Hyde and Rockton Tracts is continued.

The Sparrow Field Bird community is supported by a mixture of habitat types. The approximate proportions of habitat types as well as the current plantation rotation should be maintained. Preferred management probably means leaving the area in the existing Christmas tree crop rotation. If the trees get too large the open field species will leave. This type of management is necessary in order to prevent the overtaking of the alvar by woody growth.

Many different government agencies have policies which can affect the area of study. Detailed recommendations to each government are necessary. In order to give the reader an idea of the types of issues that arise during site management, the case study recommendations are given below.

Recommendations to the Federal Government and Union Gas Ltd
The National Government has a minor role to play on this site. It is possible that the existing high-pressure natural gas pipeline may be expanded in the future. In this eventuality the pipeline owner (Union Gas Ltd) and the approving government authority (National Energy Board) should give full recognition to the integrity of the ESA during planning, construction and maintenance. No corridor-related activities should occur outside the corridor boundaries. The maintenance of the existing pipeline corridor that crosses the ESA should emphasize native vegetation regeneration.

Recommendations to the Provincial Government
The Provincial Government has direct responsibility for natural resources and for environmental management. It has indirect control over municipalities and their operation. Therefore, three provincial agencies have a major role to play on this site. The Ministry of Natural Resources controls forest, wildlife, parks, mine and crown land management. The Ministry of Environment deals with pollution control, water management and environmental assessment. The Ministry of Housing and Municipal Affairs sets provincial municipal policy and administers plan and zoning approval.

All provincial agencies and any corporations or companies licensed or given permits by provincial authority should give full recognition to the integrity of the ESA. For example, roads and hydro-electric utility corridors should consider the integrity of the ESA during planning, construction and maintenance. No corridor-related activities should occur outside defined corridor boundaries.

The Ministry of Natural Resources should continue to manage the Hyde and Rockton Forestry Tracts in the context of its present long-term policy. Consideration must be given to the composition and structure of deciduous forests that will ultimately take the place of the existing planted coniferous forests. Attempts should be made to re-establish the indigenous oak-hickory community. Also, for those species that require upland coniferous forest, some of this community should be maintained in the long term. The existing fire ponds and wetlands system are quite important for wildlife and should not be drained or filled.

Any private landowner who requests a 50 per cent land tax rebate on his woodlot (under existing legislation) should have his request honoured if the stipulated requirements are fulfilled. This rebate has been established to encourage private woodlot retention and management (Smyth and Nausedas undated).

The existing recreational uses of hiking, hunting, horseback riding and birding are now facilitated by the presence of the two small parking lots and the trail signs as developed by the Ministry of Natural Resources. These should be maintained. The local Conservation Officer (game warden) should visit the site occasionally to ensure that hunting is done according to the existing game laws.

No quarry extraction of the limestone bedrock should be allowed within the designated ESA. The existing land uses should be encouraged to continue and major changes, such as quarry establishment, may be inappropriate.

Recommendations to the Region of Hamilton-Wentworth
This area should have high priority in the administration of the approved Official Plan designation as an ESA. The ESA boundaries as delineated in the *Ecologistics* report (1976) should be extended to include all of the Rockton Tract and the portion of sedge meadow north of and adjacent to highway No. 8 as shown in Tobias and Eagles (1977).

The Rockton and Hyde forest tracts are owned by the Region and are managed by the provincial resource agency. In its forest management agreement with the Ministry of Natural Resources, the Region should opt for a management policy that enhances habitat diversity in the forestry tracts.

With the addition of rural estate subdivisions nearby, increasing vandalism/trespass violations are possible. With these, a general environmental deterioration may occur. The Region should anticipate such problems and plan for their solution before urbanization is allowed. Subdivision location and design must be considered. The new residents should be made aware of the ecological significance of the area.

Recommendations to the Township of Flamborough
The township administers zoning by-laws and site plan review. Existing zoning by-laws should be amended in order to protect the integrity of the ESA.

Recommendations to the private landowner
Any landowner owning 10.1 ha or more of woodlot is eligible for a 50 per cent rebate of all municipal taxes directly from the Provincial Government (Smyth and Nausedas undated). The owners of woodlots should seek this rebate as remuneration for careful woodlot protection.

Any harvesting of wood should be selective in nature and should occur in the winter months. Hunting and trapping could be allowed, as long as Ontario game laws are enforced and if these activities are deemed desirable by the private landowner. If hunting is to be allowed, discretion must be used to ensure that the Upland Sandpiper is not hunted inadvertently.

All-terrain vehicles should be prohibited with the exception of snowmobiles. Snowmobiles should be restricted to the existing trails in the forestry tracts (if deemed desirable by the Region) and the open field areas of the privately-owned land (if deemed desirable by private landowners).

Active recreational activities such as snowshoeing and cross-country skiing are allowable in the forestry tracts and in the open areas of privately-owned land. Passive recreational activities need not be restricted.

Any quarrying, dumping, or filling should be prohibited. If any application of chemicals is necessary, the directions pertaining to dosage, application and disposal of containers should be carefully adhered to.

The existing Christmas tree plantations are compatible with breeding bird communities. The continual tree crop rotation is a contribution to the high bird diversity. This activity should be continued indefinitely. Care should be taken to ensure that some open field areas without trees are retained.

Restoration

Many land uses cause significant amounts of land disturbance. Is it possible to restore such derelict sites to a natural condition? Is it possible to create an Environmentally Sensitive Area on disturbed lands over time?

Many of the terrestrial ecosystems in northern temperate areas have developed on the disturbed land left by fluvioglacial activity. Each of the constituent organisms has had the dispersive capacity necessary to immigrate to the area and to colonize. It is probable that the aboriginal populations caused considerable ecosystem change, especially as agriculture developed. It is also probable that certain species were dispersed by aboriginal activity.

Man and his extensive use of technology and energy have had very large disruptive influences on the ecosystems in many parts of the world. For example, most of the southern Ontario counties at the time of European contact were covered in forest. At present the percentage of the land left in forest varies from 3 per cent in Essex County to 20 per cent in Halton County. A situation now exists which mimics to some degree the situation that occurred near the end of the last glacial period, that is, very extensive land disturbances.

Given this historical base it is reasonable to presume that a systematic programme to reclaim damaged or derelict lands is possible. Over an appropriate period it should be possible to create natural areas on those derelict lands which do not contain toxic substances that prevent growth.

Reclamation usually refers to the act of returning a derelict landscape to a form that is useful for a purpose such as urban, agricultural or forestry use. Restoration refers to the act of returning a derelict landscape to a state that is a functioning natural ecosystem. In this section, the word restoration is used because I see the end point as being the creation of a natural biological community on previously derelict land.

McLellan (1973) found that 1,170 ha of land in the Waterloo Region of Ontario were in a derelict state. Of this area, 78 per cent had been used for surface mining. McLellan, Yundt and Dorfman (1979) found that a further 2,415 ha were licensed for surface mining. Therefore, 3,585 ha of land were or soon would be in a derelict state. This compares to the 7,871 ha of land (Francis 1977) that had been designated as environmentally sensitive in the Regional Official Plan. Therefore, 5.85 per cent of the Waterloo Region is in a designated ESA condition while 2.67 per cent is in a derelict or licensed mining condition.

In Canada, the movement to reclaim derelict land has only got under way in the last 10 years. Most of the efforts have been aimed at the reclamation or sequential use of surface mining sites. In Ontario, attempts have been made to reclaim surface mining sites for cattle pasture (Stratton 1979), recreational lakes (Mulamootil and Farvolden 1975), golf courses and fishing ponds (Anonymous 1978b) or just to establish vegetative cover (Coates 1976). In Hamilton, the Royal Botanical Gardens established a very successful botanical garden in an abandoned quarry. In one interesting case, the Leslie Street Spit in Toronto, the creation of new terrestrial habitat by landfill inadvertently created a significant breeding area for gulls and terns in Lake Ontario (Temple 1980). This circumstance had not been consciously planned. The establishment of an ecological management and monitoring project in a derelict gravel pit south of Guelph, Ontario, was the one of the first of its kind in Canada. Results from this study have shown that gravel pits have the potential for reclamation to a relatively natural ecological condition in southern Ontario (Eagles 1982; Eagles and Gewurz 1982).

In Great Britain the range expansion of the Little Ringed Plover due to the breeding habitat provided by gravel pits alerted many people to the possibility of the use of old pits and quarries for natural area purposes (Milne 1974). Extensive inventory work has now been done on the biological communities that exist on derelict lands (Glue 1970: Milne 1974: Catchpole and Tydeman 1975). Emphasis has been placed on those areas that are mined below the water table and create a habitat for wetland community development.

In 1956 an experiment was started in a flooded gravel pit in west Kent, England, with the intention of creating a wetland community. By 1967 the reclamation had been so successful that the area was designated a Site of Special Scientific Interest by the Nature Conservancy under section 23 of the National Parks and Access to the Countryside Act (Harrison and Harrison

1972, 1976). In 15 seasons of measurement the waterfowl population increased by over 50 per cent. The peak waterfowl usage per day increased from 6,253 in 1956–57 to a peak of 100,438 in 1969–70. Breeding bird censuses recorded an increase from 281 pairs of 40 species to a peak of 1,300 pairs of 55 species. In all 189 species of birds were recorded on the reserve. The increases were ascribed to the habitat construction carried out in the early stages and to the planting of 18,707 food and cover plants. All of this work was carried out by a team of 12 volunteers, all working in their spare time (Harrison and Harrison 1972).

Street (1982) suggested that the gravel industry in Great Britain is creating new freshwater wetlands in the process of excavating below the water table. The Great Linford Gravel Quarry project in central England is an attempt by a gravel producer to establish an extensive waterfowl breeding and research area in an operating pit. Even after only 11 years of operation the project has had considerable success in establishing significant populations of breeding waterfowl as well as large flocks of wintering birds.

A number of studies in the United States have shown the viability of the concept of reclaiming derelict lands for wildlife purposes. The Max McGraw Wildlife Foundation is supervising the extraction and reclamation of gravel lands in Kane County, Illinois for fish and wildlife purposes (Oldenburg *et al.* 1982). Restoration projects with an emphasis on the creation of natural ecosystems have also taken place in Fort Collins, Colorado (Alden 1982), near Sibley, Louisiana (Ettinger and Yuill 1982), on the coastal plains of New Jersey (Lomax 1982) and in northern Minnesota (Svedarsky 1982). The recent research in this field in the United States has shown conclusively that some types of derelict lands can be reclaimed relatively quickly. Swanson (1982) has made a number of detailed recommendations, based on past research experience in the US, concerning the appropriate site, design and management policies necessary for the development of maximum habitat and species diversity.

The success of the activities in Great Britain and the United States and the increasing acreages of derelict land everywhere suggest that the reclamation of lands for natural purposes is a reasonable possibility. It is essential that policies for the preservation of natural ecological diversity look at the possibilities of creating new natural areas in addition to protecting those that now exist (Dorney 1975). Dorney (1977b) has outlined a checklist of points to be considered during the design of a mini-ecosystem for natural area purposes (Table 5.3).

Gardeners have developed many techniques for the transplantation and growth of native plants. The earliest approach was to transplant single, showy plants into a typical flower garden. In the last decade many impressive recreations of natural ecosystems have been constructed (Kramer 1973; Hull 1976; Crockett and Allen 1977). A melding of the concepts inherent in native plant gardening and landscape architecture is quickly developing pragmatic approaches to the design and construction of natural landscapes (Diek-

Table 5.3 Design guidelines for mini-ecosystems

Dorney (1975) outlined the development of a small prairie/oak forest ecosystem in the front yard of a suburban house. Subsequent experimentation on a number of areas resulted in the development of a set of design guidelines that can be used for the development of small forest ecosystems (Dorney 1977b). These guidelines are as follows:

1. A tight vertical shrub and herbaceous edge 'skin' needs to be protected or developed, particularly on southerly and westerly exposures, to control growth and invasion of grass and weeds.
2. Paths, walkways, service lines, roads, etc., should enter and exit on the cooler, northerly or easterly edges where possible. This controls weeds and grassy invasion.
3. Minimum depth is 9 ft if a tree-shrub-herbaceous association is to be formed, 6 ft if only shrubs and herbaceous flora are used.
4. Shrubs and trees that can clone (such as dogwood, aspen, pin cherry) should be preferred within the outer 6 to 9 ft of edge.
5. A combination of pioneer and mid-successional tree species can be planted concurrently; species which form the regional climax should not be relied upon at the outset.
6. The tree species selected should be suitable for the site region with due consideration given to climates, soil type and soil moisture. A climatic evaluation, a soil survey and knowledge of local plant communities will determine which plant system to select and its appropriate successional dynamics.
7. Limiting factors (present and future) such as salt spray, air pollution, rabbit and mice populations should be studied and more resistant species selected.
8. Weed by-laws must be followed.
9. Hazardous or poisonous plants should be avoided or removed.
10. Fire hazard must be evaluated.
11. Access to easements, including overhead wires, must be maintained.
12. Visibility for safety considerations at intersections should be maintained.
13. Scale of planting in relation to the lot and building size should be evaluated.
14. Functional benefits and disbenefits of the planting for wind control, snow control, erosion control, runoff reduction, or as a nutrient sink, should be evaluated.
15. Amenity value for colour, sound, odour should be planned.
16. Wildlife potential for nesting and feeding of reptiles, mammals and birds should be planned.
17. Vandalism difficulties should be anticipated.
18. Allelopathic (toxic) effects should be minimized.
19. Flowering date considerations should be part of the design process.
20. Edible plants (trees, shrubs and herbs) can be selected.
21. Plant species symbolic to certain ethnic groups should be understood.
22. Soil fertility and pH must be suitable for species selected, augmented by commercial fertilizer in the first few years.
23. Microdrainage on the site must not be altered unless added moisture can be utilized by the plant system developed.
24. Existing stands can be pre-stressed prior to development to encourage growth and those species able to cope with the new environment.
25. Linkage of the area to other larger scale natural features should be considered.
26. Annuals may be considered for the initial planting to give the area more colour and appeal.

elmann and Schuster 1982). Many of the necessary techniques are now available for the restoration of plant communities on derelict sites.

Summary

It is essential that site management take place in ESAs. Some sites may be better off left alone. Others may require a buffering of human impacts and uses. Still others may require active manipulation. The exact needs of a site must be determined based upon an inventory of the resources as well as recognition of the role of this site with the overall ESA system.

One of the reasons for protecting ESAs is the need to conserve genetic resources for the reclamation of disturbed lands. The restoration of derelict lands to a natural ecological state has been undertaken with considerable success in a number of countries. It is possible to manage derelict sites so that ecological succession takes place. This may be a management consideration both within and adjacent to existing ESAs.

CHAPTER 6

Selected case studies

Introduction

The planning and management of natural landscapes at the local governmental level is probably best understood by reference to specific examples. In this chapter, county-level case studies are examined from four different countries: Great Britain, Japan, Canada and the United States.

Great Britain and Japan are old countries with rich and complex cultural histories. Their landscapes have been extensively utilized and modified over centuries of human occupation. Agriculture and urbanization have been major ecosystem modifiers for long periods. It can also be said, with some justification, that both countries have a tradition of sensitivity to the natural environment.

Canada and the United States are young countries with fairly recent cultural traditions. The previous native populations have been almost completely removed and been replaced by settlers of European extraction. In just a few centuries a very major landscape modification has occurred as much of the natural ecosystem has been replaced by agricultural and urban systems.

The County of Gwent in southern Wales, the Wakayama prefecture on Honshu, Halton County in Ontario and Montgomery County in Maryland are the locations of the case studies. Each have their unique attributes, but in general they represent the countries in which they are located.

Great Britain

Introduction

Great Britain contains England, Scotland, Wales and Northern Ireland with a population approaching 56 million in 1980, on a relatively small area of

85

244,044 sq./km. It is an old country with a long tradition of intensive land use and management. Britain is one of the world's leading industrialized nations.

Agricultural activities have taken place for thousands of years. Urbanization and industrialization have been a major component of the community structure for hundreds of years. As a result, very little and possibly none of the country could be considered to lack human influence. The fields, forests, cities, moors and seashores comprise a complex cultural landscape that has evolved slowly through thousands of years of human-nature interaction.

In Great Britain, as in most of Europe, the length and intensity of land settlement has resulted in the loss of most of the natural vegetation, especially in the form of large contiguous blocks. That which remains is located in fragmented locations that are usually infertile, remote, inaccessible or thinly populated. Therefore the establishment of national parks based upon the North American model, that is, large undisturbed areas, is an impossibility. Efforts must be concentrated on smaller areas (Poore 1981).

The majority of the soils suitable for agriculture have been cleared for that purpose. Natural vegetation is still found on steep slopes, in valleys and in wetlands. Nevertheless, the traditional farming techniques usually ensured that a diversity of fields, hedges, waterways and woods existed in the rural areas (Mabey 1980).

Since the Second World War large-scale changes have been taking place in the ancient pastoral landscape. In a fashion similar to North America, the agricultural development has concentrated on larger farms with fewer owners. The intensive use of energy, usually of a fossil fuel origin, and heavy equipment has dictated an enlargement of field size. This has resulted in the clearance of thousands of kilometres of hedges and hundreds of small woods. In central England where the relatively flat land encourages agricultural development the change has resulted in the loss of many species of wildlife, as clearly illustrated by the findings of the *Atlas of the Bumblebees* (IBRA 1980). Figure 6.1 shows that *Bombus humilis* has largely disappeared from agricultural central England.

Goode (undated) has shown that the overall trend of landscape alteration has been towards agricultural development at the expense of wildlife and its habitat (Fig. 6.2). Extensive areas of heathland have been converted to intensive agriculture, as in Dorset where only 15 per cent remains compared to that present in 1760. An associated species, the Sand Lizard (*Lacenta agilis*), has declined by 74 per cent in its distribution in southern England. In the north of England and Scotland, of the original area of the lowland raised bogs only 13 per cent remains. The grasslands are easily converted to arable land, as shown in Dorset where 72 per cent had been destroyed by 1972. The Snakeshead Fritillary butterfly, an old meadow species, declined from 116 atlas (10 km) squares to only 15 in southern England between 1950

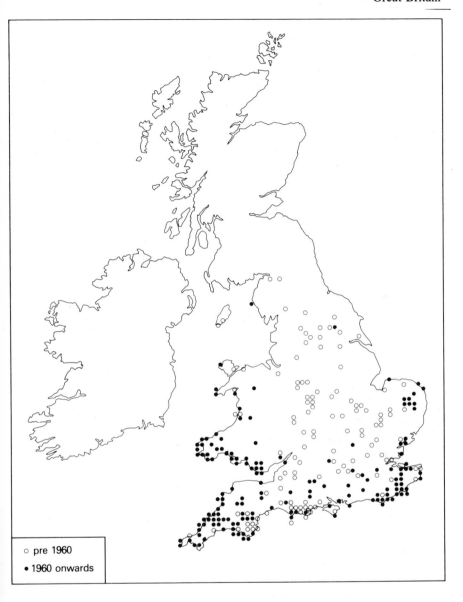

Figure 6.1 Atlas of a bumblebee (*Bombus humilis*) for Great Britain.   The distribution of this bumblebee shows the range contraction that has occurred since 1960. The hollow circles show occurrences before 1960 while the closed circles show records after 1960. Central England has undergone forest and hedgerow clearance on a massive scale thereby removing the habitat for many species. This humble insect is a good indicator of this extensive wildlife habitat loss.
Source: International Bee Research Association 1980

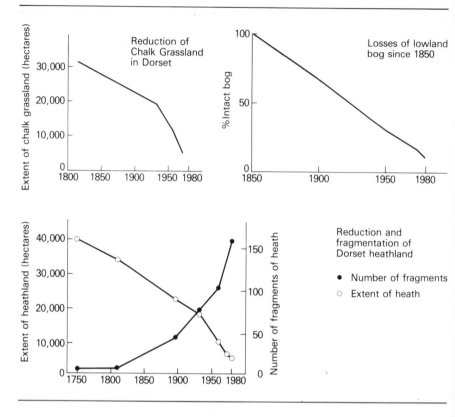

Figure 6.2 Habitat losses in Britain. The dramatic decrease of natural biological communities is clearly evident in these graphs.
Source: Goode (undated) and Goode 1981

to 1981. Even the deciduous woodlands have been cleared and some estimates state that between 30 and 50 per cent of all such woodland in Britain has been lost since 1947 (Goode undated). Similarly in Scotland, woodland has decreased by 56 per cent since the Second World War.

Goode's summary illustrates the tragic and accelerating loss of natural ecosystems in Great Britain. Several private conservation groups and the government are now undertaking initiatives to protect a minimum representative area of each habitat type before it is all removed.

The small size of the country and the extensive amount of landscape alteration has dictated that the standard model of national park cannot be applied. Large undisturbed areas do not occur, so other forms of protection have had to be developed.

National parks in Great Britain are cultural landscapes usually with an above normal proportion of natural areas. They are governed by appointed committees with both local and national representation. The vast majority of the land within the park is in private ownership and the residents carry on their normal activities (Simmons 1978). In structure these park committees are actually regional planning commissions similar to the Niagara Escarpment Commission in Ontario, the Adirondacks Park Agency (1979a and b, 1980) in New York State and the California Coastal Planning Commission (Hill 1982). In all of these situations an appointed board has been given statutory obligations to make and enforce rules for the careful management of public and private lands within a designated feature of environmental significance.

To protect and maintain a representative set of ecological communities and their corresponding flora and fauna, a National Nature Reserve system has been started. Ratcliffe (1977, p. 3), in his monumental work that outlined an inventory of the most important areas for nature conservation, stated that:

It is now accepted that human impact in Britain is so universal and pervasive that no area of land or water is safe from developments destructive or deleterious to their nature conservation interest, unless deliberate measures are taken to ensure that they remain unmodified.

The first step has been the national inventory of sites worthy of protection. Ratcliffe (1977) listed some 700 sites that comprise a system with representation of all important ecosystem types in the country. Then a national series of key sites were selected so that conservation effort could be concentrated on the most important sites. Four hundred of the sites (670,000 ha) were classified as Grade 1, which means of national or international importance. Approximately 20 per cent of these Grade 1 sites are already National Nature Reserves (Poore and Gryn-Ambroes 1980). Grade 2 sites were also of national significance but either duplicated Grade 1 sites or were of lower quality. The 300 Grade 2 sites cover 280,000 ha. All Grade 1 and 2 sites were scheduled as Sites of Special Scientific Interest (SSSIs) by the Nature Conservancy Council. These SSSI's contain the nationally important Grade 1 and 2 sites as well as hundreds of others that are usually of regional or local significance. Finally, a long-term ongoing programme has been undertaken to develop protection measures for the key sites. Some have been purchased by the national government or a private conservation group such as The National Trust, the County Trusts for Nature Conservation, and the Royal Society for the Protection of Birds. On others, management agreements have been signed with private owners. In others, open conflicts of opinion rage as the owners indicate a desire to destroy the ecological features so that the site can be used for some other purpose.

The Nature Conservancy Council administered 161 National Nature Reserves with a total area of 126,246 ha as of June 1978 in England, Scotland and Wales (Poore and Gryn-Ambroes 1980). Only 26 per cent of this was owned by the national government. Thirteen per cent was under a Nature Reserve Agreement with the owner and 61 per cent was leased from private landowners. Local governments had established 56 Local Nature

Reserves with an area of 7,129 ha. In addition private organizations, such 'as the Royal Society for the Protection of Nature Reserves, have established reserves totalling over 62,000 ha. Over 3,600 sites of special scientific interest have been identified by the Nature Conservancy Council. The vast majority of these are in private ownership, with local planning authorities having a major role to play in their future.

In Northern Ireland there were 31 National Nature Reserves covering 2,975 ha in 1978. The Nature Reserves Committee has suggested that 60 more nature reserves and 100 Areas of Scientific Interest be protected (Poore and Gryn-Ambroes 1980).

This nature reserve system is continually evolving and improving. What separates it from most North American systems is the degree of emphasis placed on the use of cooperative landowner agreements as well as the excellent nation-wide inventory that can be used to priorize the sites.

Institutional environment

Great Britain is a constitutional monarchy with a powerful central government. The national government has authority over natural resources and municipal governments. The 1971 Town and Country Planning Act lays down the ground rules for local government planning.

Municipalities develop Structure Plans that outline a general set of planning policies. These plans do not distinguish individual properties or show the effect of policies on specific properties of land. The intent is to develop a strategy for the entire area.

> The essential role of the structure plan is to set out – against the background of economic and social considerations – physical, transportation and environmental policies and proposals for the area covered (Department of the Environment 1973, p. 3).

The Secretary of State for the Environment approves the plan, except in Wales where the Secretary of State for Wales gives the approval. After approval, local plans will be developed in detail for particular areas within the framework of the Structure Plan (DOE 1972; DOE 1973). Local plans need only be approved by the local planning authority, which is usually a county council.

The National Parks and Access to the Countryside Act 1949 allows the Nature Conservancy Council to establish National Nature Reserves and to schedule Sites of Special Scientific Interest (SSSIs). The Nature Conservancy Council has the mandate for nature conservation. It does not have the responsibility for forestry, hunting, fishing or mining as is so often the case in North American resource management agencies. The Countryside Commission for England and Wales was established by the 1949 Act and provides for the establishment of National Parks. The Act was amended in 1972, enabling county councils to establish Local Nature Reserves. The

The Long-eared Owl (*Asio otus*) is circumpolar in northern temperate climes. This woodland species is nowhere common and has restricted amounts of habitat due to the scarcity of forest in settled areas. The continual loss of natural habitat due to agricultural intensification and urban development affects this and many other forest dwelling species.

Local Government Act for Scotland 1973 set up similar arrangements in Scotland.

The Countryside Act 1968 allows the establishment of Country Parks, which are small picnic and camping sites. The Town and Country Planning Act governs the development of Structure Plans by municipalities. These are often called Official Plans in Canada and Master Plans in the United States. Nature conservation is one element to be taken into account in the creation of Structure Plans. The 1968 Countryside Act and the 1967 Scotland Countryside Act dictate that municipalities and other public agencies must have regard to the desirability of conserving flora, fauna, geological and physiographic features during the exercise of their duties in regards to land.

The Nature Conservancy Council is required by legislation to identify SSSIs and to notify the local authority of their existence. These local government agencies are in turn required to consult the Nature Conservancy Council if there is an application to alter the use of land that is an SSSI. Land drainage, tree planting, pasture tillage and most agricultural activities are not legally considered to be land uses and therefore no notification need take place. Many old pasture or moor SSSIs have been destroyed by agricultural practises without the knowledge of the Nature Conservancy Council.

In Great Britain, SSSIs are not designated but the Planning Authority and the landowner are merely notified in writing by the Nature Conservancy Council that the sites exist. Consultation procedures are set up. If there is a conflict between the Nature Conservancy Council and the local Planning Authority over granting planning approval for development on or near the site, the application has to be sent to the relevant Secretary of State for adjudication. Local Authorities can assist in the protection of recognized SSSIs by:

1. Policies and general proposals within a Structure Plan.
2. Delineation on the proposals Map of a Local Plan together with associated policies.
3. The development of regional policies.
4. The preparation of a special plan dealing with this topic.
5. The designation of Local Nature Reserves together with a Management Plan which can be implemented by purchase or lease of the land or by a formal contractual agreement.
6. Purchase (Sprott pers. comm.).

The last two options are expensive and are seldom used.

Most of the counties, such as Gwent to be discussed below, rely on the inventories done by the national government agency, the Nature Conservancy Council, for site definition and mapping. The Grampian Region Council in Scotland, however, has taken the initiative itself in studying the Environmentally Sensitive Areas of Grampian County. These ESAs are found in one of three categories: natural science, built environment and natural resources. The sites of interest to natural science are those of importance in the fields of geology, geomorphology, entomology, botany, ornithology, fresh water biology and nature conservation. The built environment category contains historic buildings, field monuments and archaeological sites as well as sites for historic conservation. Natural resources mapping was done for distinctive scenic landscapes, high-class agricultural land, woodland and forest zones as well as sand and gravel deposits (Sprott 1977). This inclusion of significant natural areas, cultural artifacts and natural resources such as soils and aggregate deposits is different from the situation in Canada where the words Environmentally Sensitive Area would refer to the significant natural areas alone.

The inventory in Scotland of the sites of interest to natural history was compiled by faculty members from a number of departments at Aberdeen University (Grampian Regional Council 1980). The use of expert advice from nearby universities is a widespread technique in Britain. It has proved effective elsewhere too, such as in the Region of Waterloo in Ontario (Eagles 1979).

The County of Gwent, Wales

Introduction
The county of Gwent is located in southern Wales (Fig. 6.3). The County of Monmouthshire was formed in 1536 and was renamed Gwent in 1974 along with a number of boundary changes. The county covers 386,685 ha

Figure 6.3 Location of the County of Gwent, Wales

and had a population of 438,000 in 1980 (Nature Conservancy Council undated a).

The county borders on the Severn Estuary to the south; the English counties of Gloucestershire, Herefordshire and Worcestershire to the east, the Welsh county of Powys in the north as well as Mid and South Glamorgan to the west. The area is strategically located between England and Wales and had a long tradition of warfare with invading Romans, Danes, Normans and English. The extensive coal deposits have resulted in densely populated industrial valleylands in the northern portion of the county.

The coalfield extends across southern Wales in an old geological basin with coal measures lining the centre. The coal mining resulted in the construction of steel mills and other associated industries. Many manufacturing plants have been built (Ferriday 1961).

The natural environment
The county is bordered by the Black Mountains of Powys to the north and the Old Red Sandstone Marls of Herefordshire and Worcestershire to the north-east. These uplands reach a height of 596 m on Sugar Loaf Mountain, with extensive moorlands developed on the hill tops and upper valley slopes. The moors are open grasslands that are kept cropped by continuous sheep grazing. In the valleys deciduous woodlands occur. Mixed farmland with high hedges and small woods occupy the valleys. The uplands and steep valleys of the north and west contrast to the low hills of the centre and east and the flat coastal plain to the south (Fig. 6.4).

The western coalfields are found in a series of industrialized valleys that run southward from the northern mountains. The eastern half of the county is a complex series of pastoral landscapes with villages, farms, lanes and woodlands. The coastal lowlands in the south border the Severn Estuary.

The coal and other developments of the western valleys resulted in the construction of active, industrial towns with the concurrent destruction of the hardwood forests for fuel and lumber. In recent decades, urban expansion has continued and new steelworks and an expressway have been constructed. Many small villages have grown considerably and coniferous forests have been planted in place of the former deciduous woodlands. Agricultural intensification has caused the removal of many hedgerows and small woodlots.

Gwent contains a portion of the Brecon Beacons National Park (Fig. 6.5) and the Wye Valley Area of Outstanding Natural Beauty, both of which are designated by the national government under the authority of the National Parks and Access to the Countryside Act 1940.

This county in southern Wales has warm summers with mild winters. The average daily high in July is 15 degrees C, while in January it is a mild 5 degrees C. In total 100 cm of precipitation falls in the south while up to 250 cm can fall in the northern mountains. From 170 to 225 days with rain occur as one moves inland to the uplands. Snow occasionally falls on the highlands (Drury 1973).

Gwent has an estimated 18,210 ha of woodland which amounts to 13 per cent of the total county land area. This is higher than elsewhere, as Wales has an average of only 10 per cent and Britain an average of 8 per cent (Probert 1978). The natural broadleaved forests are composed of oak, beech, ash and birch trees while the plantations contain a variety of imported
94

Figure 6.4 A Satellite Photograph of Southern Wales including the County of Gwent. This ERTS image taken on February 14, 1976 shows southern Wales and part of southwestern England. The rugged, mountainous interior of Wales contrasts to the rolling countryside along the coast of the Bristol Channel and Severn Estuary. The Black Mountains in northern Gwent and southern Powys Counties contain significant remnant natural areas due to past land uses and the presence of areas not intensively cultivated or urbanized.

conifers. Approximately 10 per cent of the county is common land and is used mainly for sheep grazing but is increasingly the location of a variety of outdoor recreation activities such as walking, pony trekking, field sports and picnicking. These activities are most often not strictly legal but are tolerated by the farmers who own the common grazing rights.

Policies

The Nature Conservancy Council (undated b) has published a document that maps and describes all the significant environment sites in Gwent (Fig. 6.6).

Figure 6.5 Black Mountains in Brecon Beacons National Park.   The Welsh mountains are havens for many species of wildlife because of the natural ecosystems remaining on steep slopes and at high altitudes. The commons and moors are often extensive pieces of seminatural vegetation.

These include National Nature Reserves and Sites of Special Scientific Interest.

The County of Gwent Structure Plan was adopted by the county council in 1976 and approved by the Secretary of State for Wales in 1981. Therefore the plan has legal force.

The Plan is composed of two documents. The Report of Survey outlines issues and presents background and inventory data. It is a statement of fact only and is not given formal approval. The Written Statement of Policies and Proposals contains policies dealing with issues such as: existing national policies that impact the County, employment, housing and settlement, environmental improvement, countryside resources, transportation, utilities and community facilities. Detailed policies that are relevant to the protection of local natural areas are given below (Bray and Probert 1981).

> The county council will in co-operation with the Nature Conservancy Council recognize and define nature conservation sites that are of national, regional and local interest, and identify and define areas within the county to reflect the variety and scarcity of flora and fauna and geological and geomorphological interests. Measures will be taken to ensure proper protection and management of nature conservation sites and areas so that scientific and educational interests are safeguarded (p. 120).

Figure 6.6 Special environmental sites of the County of Gwent.   These natural
biological communities are forests, moors, river valleys and an estuary. These
represent the most significant natural biological communities remaining in the
county. Two levels of significance are shown. National Nature Reserve and Site of
Special Scientific Interest.
Source: Nature Conservancy Council (undated (b))

There will be a presumption against further new quarries or substantial
extensions to existing quarries within the Brecon Beacons National
Park, the Wye Valley Area of Outstanding Natural Beauty and Defined

Special Landscape Areas unless the planning authority is satisfied that it is in the national interest (p. 102).

Characteristic and individual landscape types throughout the County will be protected and conserved as 'Special Landscape Areas' (SLAs) for the purposes of controlling and regulating the effects of urban and industrial development: resolving the conflicts between agricultural, recreational, and forestry/woodland interests; protecting and improving landscape and wildlife resources (p. 119).

Within the Brecon Beacons National Park and Wye Valley Area of Outstanding Natural Beauty and other protected areas there will be a presumption against the establishment of outdoor recreational or tourist facilities which might more properly be located elsewhere in the County particularly in recreational and amenity areas as indicated in the area statements (p. 125).

Problems and successes

These generally-worded policies appear to give a measure of protection to the SSSIs. The general wording of the statement; 'Measures will be taken to ensure proper protection and management. . .', suggests that the county is leaving much of the detailed protection and management work to the Nature Conservancy Council. The definition of what constitutes 'measures' is not obvious but practice suggests that it is a virtual prohibition of land development (housing, industry, extraction) but allows land-use alteration such as agricultural clearance or forest management.

The Gwent Structure Plan is one example of the relatively close national and local government cooperation that takes place with regard to nature conservation. The undertaking of inventory work and conservation initiative by the national government is significant in that it demonstrates to the municipalities that the issue is of national concern. This situation is not to be found in the United States or Canada, where the national governments have little or no communication with municipalities.

One important institution is the placement of conservation planners throughout the nation in a series of offices of the Nature Conservancy Council. These people provide advice on a wide variety of issues including the planning and management of SSSIs. Their presence also enables a central agency to keep watch over the planning and management of significant natural landscapes in local municipalities.

The SSSI notification procedure and the cooperation of local counties have been largely effective in protecting the SSSIs from small-scale residential, commercial and industrial projects. Large-scale projects of national importance have been able to overrule SSSI concerns in a number of locales. The biggest failure has been the inability of the existing institutions to halt the negative impact of forestry and agriculture. Goode (1981) has shown that lowland fields and forests are disappearing at an alarming rate both within and outside SSSIs. The attempts to place forestry and agricultural land changes under municipal planning control during the 1981 revisions to ↓ Wildlife and Countryside Act failed. As a result this trend will continu unless SSSIs are protected by a stronger designation and land-use alteration limitation. Notification has been effective in the majority of cases each year but the minority of losses are impossible to replace.

On the surface the simple act of notification appears to give little protection to a natural site. The reasons for the effectiveness must be in the widespread public acceptance of government regulation and in the very strong environmental movement. Great Britain has one of the largest, if not the largest, number of naturalists in the world. These people are interested in exploring and learning in the natural environment. Their numbers, status in society and knowledge provide an important force for protective policies.

Conclusions

Great Britain has a very long history of active and intensive use of the land by large numbers of people. Nevertheless, many natural biological communities remain in protected areas and many wild species have slowly adapted to the changing conditions and have survived.

In the last three decades, rapid and large-scale landscape alterations have occurred, largely the result of agricultural and forestry intensification. This has created a critical situation where many habitat types and wild species have become rare and on the verge of extirpation. The nation-wide conservation effort has involved careful national inventories (Perring and Walters 1962; Sharrock 1976; Ratcliffe 1977), land purchase and landowner agreements for National Nature Reserves and designation of SSSIs.

Research by the Nature Conservancy Council has shown that the loss of landscape and ecological diversity continues. Up to 10 per cent of SSSIs have their nature conservation value removed annually. The losses due to typical urban and industrial developments have largely been eliminated – it is intensive agricultural and forestry management that is causing the damage. The situation is well recognized by conservation interests in Great Britain and it is probable that the pressure will soon build up again on the national law makers for a legal remedy to the problem.

Japan

Introduction

Japan is an old country with a long developmental history. It is 377,440 sq. km in size with over 115,000,000 residents in 1980. The population density is surpassed by only a few countries such as Belgium, Holland and South Korea. Japan consists of four main islands and hundreds of smaller ones scattered in a chain along the western Pacific rim. The islands are characterized by impressive interior mountains, short rushing rivers, forested slopes, interior lakes and restricted agricultural plains. With only 20 per cent of the land arable, development has concentrated in the coastal and inland plains.

Japan was the first Asian country to successfully challenge the domination of the European powers when it defeated Russia in the beginning of the twentieth century. This occurred during the rapid climb of the country from a feudal state to a modern country. Japan was the first Asian country to industrialize, which it did in a very rapid fashion.

The large population and small land area has resulted in intense agricultural development. Even marginal areas such as mountain slopes and river valleys are utilized for farming.

The country has a high ecological diversity due to its 15 degrees of latitude spread from north to south along with the altitudinal variation from sea level to mountain top. Over 9,000 species of vascular plants occur. The flora forms a temperate zone forest with boreal forests in the north and at higher elevations in the south. Subtropical ecosystems occupy the extreme south.

Although small with a high population, Japan retains considerable natural value with 68 per cent of the total land area covered by forest. Japan has the highest percentage of its land in forest of any major country in the world (Yano 1978). This high figure is made up of 20.8 per cent in planted forest, 21 per cent in second growth forest, 4.5 per cent in second growth forest that has low evidence of human influence and 21.7 per cent of naturally-grown forest. In addition, native grasslands cover 1.1 per cent of the nation. Corresponding to this is 3.1 per cent in urban development and 16 per cent in farmland. The coast is an attraction for people but nevertheless 59.6 per cent of Japan's coastline is considered to be in a virgin state.

Of the total forest area of Japan, 57 per cent is on private land while 32 per cent is owned by the national government and 11 per cent by the municipalities. Much of the government-held forest has been handed down from past times before the rights of private ownership had been established by law. Since the late 1950s the national and prefectural governments have been actively pursuing reforestation policies (Gorrie 1969).

The land area covered by forests increased from 25.16 m. hectares in 1965 to 25.23 m. hectares in 1972. In the same period farmland decreased from 6.43 to 5.99 m. hectares (Japan Environment Agency 1976a). These data were derived from a national census of vegetation that was mapped on a basis of 360,000, one-kilometre grid squares on a scale of 1: 50,000. This survey is conducted at five-year intervals (Japan Environment Agency 1976b) and the latest one was 1978/79 (Japan National Tourist Organization 1981).

This large amount of natural vegetation is quite remarkable given the population density of the country. The many mountainous areas are a considerable impediment to land use and thereby retain natural vegetation.

100

The Shinto faith emphasizes nature worship and the care of natural areas. Many natural areas survive as the location of shrines. Shinto shrines and Buddhist temples are surrounded by holy forest. Woods and large trees are seen as objects to be respected and feared. The dense evergreen forest at shrines provides a respectful natural environment for worship. In the past entry to the shrine woods was prohibited and today many people are still afraid of violating them. Traditionally during the harvesting of trees in any woods a religious ceremony was performed before and after the cutting (Taoda 1982). As stated by the Japan Environment Agency (1977, p. 23);

it has been our unique cultural tradition that man, nature and man's works of art form an organic unity. In view of this part played by nature in our social life, it might be said with reason that we must in the first place appreciate highly the value of nature and make a spirit of protection and conservation our daily rule.

Institutional environment

In Asia, Japan has the longest history of parliamentary government. In 1885, a parliament was created by edict of the emperor. After the Second World War the governmental structure was completely changed with the development of a democratic government at three levels (national, prefectural, municipal). The constitution and government are based upon a combination of the British and American systems (Mukherjee 1966).

There are two local government tiers, the prefecture and the municipality. The prefecture is analogous to the county in the US and Canada. It is not as influential in politics or as large in area as states or provinces. Each of the 46 prefectures is governed by a governor and a single-house legislature. Each of 578 cities, 2,013 towns and 684 villages elect their own mayors and councils. All the territory in a prefecture is also included within one of the lower-level municipal units (McNelly 1972).

During the US occupation a strong attempt was made to decentralize political power and strengthen democracy at the local governmental levels. Accordingly, when the new constitution was adopted in 1946 a general principle was established that local governments should be autonomous bodies and democratically elected.

The relevant sections of the constitution that deal with local self-government are (Mukherjee 1966):

Article 92 Regulations concerning organization and operations of local public entities shall be fixed by law in accordance with the principles of local autonomy.

Article 93 The local public entities shall establish assemblies as their deliberature organs, in accordance with law. The chief executive officers of all local public entities, the members of the assemblies, and such local officials as may be determined by law shall be elected by direct vote within their several communities.

Article 94 Local public entities shall have the right to manage their property, affairs and administration and to enact their own regulations within law.

Article 95 A special law applicable to one local public entity cannot be enacted by the Diet without the Consent of the majority of the voters of the local public entity concerned, obtained in accordance with law.

Article 94 states that local public entities have the right to manage their property, affairs and administration and to enact their own regulations; but no precise functions or powers of local governments are given in the constitution so therefore these powers are delegated to them by the national parliament – the Diet. The Local Autonomy Law was passed by the national government in 1947. It outlines the powers given to the local governments. Among others, these include: policing, education, protection of health and safety of local inhabitants, establishment and management of parks, museums, land reclamation, zoning and coordination of activities with other local bodies. However, the national government may also deal with any of these issues if it so decides, which often results in overlap and jurisdictional dispute. Any special law that concerns one local government specifically cannot be passed by the Diet without the consent of the majority of voters in the local public entity concerned.

The national government has much more tax-raising ability than does local government and therefore must give substantial grants to keep the local levels functioning. This fiscal power gives the upper level much control over local programmes. Since 1947 strong centralization pressures from the central government have reduced local government influence.

Individuals have the right of owning property under Article 29 of the constitution. Achieving a balance between private property rights and public welfare is a major issue, as in the other democratic countries discussed in these case studies. Article 29 states that (Ukai and Nathanson 1968):

The right to own or hold property is inviolable.

Property rights shall be defined by law, in conformity with the public welfare.

Private property may be taken for public use upon just compensation therefor.

The rapid economic growth of Japan has been accompanied by environmental degradation. The increase in income and leisure time of the populace has created a strong demand for outdoor recreation in relatively unspoiled environments. The Japanese Government has developed a tourism policy that attempts to accomplish two possibly conflicting goals – the conservation of the natural environment and its use for recreation. In 1977, the Third Comprehensive National Development Plan was approved by the Japanese Cabinet. One of its goals was the maintenance of approximately 600,000 ha of land as undeveloped wild nature where the only use would be scientific research and limited outdoor recreation. In addition, up to 6,000,000 ha of land would be used as parks where facilities would be allowed as long as the environmental impact was minimal (Japan National Tourist Organization 1981).

Japan has six parks systems: National Parks, Quasi-National Parks, Prefectural Natural Parks, Prefectural Nature Conservation Areas, Nature Conservation Areas and Wilderness Areas. The first three categories are generally known as natural parks. Their planning and management are governed by the Natural Parks Law and the Nature Conservation Law of 1972 (Japan National Tourist Organization 1981). In addition, Wildlife Protection Areas have been established.

There are 27 National Parks (2,020,460 ha) covering 5.35 per cent of the country (Table 6.1). They are usually chosen because of outstanding natural beauty and may not necessarily be environmentally sensitive or of scientific interest (Patterson pers. comm.). They are designated by the Director General of the Environment Agency on the basis of the opinion of the independent advisory body, the Nature Conservation Council. An administrative control is imposed on all land within these parks in order to protect their natural beauty. The zoning system is used regardless of land ownership. Any act which might damage the scenery of the National Park is forbidden. This

Table 6.1 Protected natural area in Japan

Category	Number of areas	Area in ha	Percentage of country
National Park[1]	27	2,020,460	5.35
Quasi-National Park[1]	51	1,147,201	3.04
Prefectural Nature Park[1]	293	2,045,234	5.42
Prefectural Nature Conservation Areas[1]	427	76,334	0.20
Nature Conservation Areas[1]	6	4,889	0.01
Wilderness Areas[1]	5	5,631	0.01
Wildlife Protection Areas[2] (National Government)	524	1,061,000	2.81
Wildlife Protection Areas[2] (Prefectures)	2,251	1,543,000	4.08
Totals	3,584	7,903,749	20.92

1 Japan National Tourist Organization 1981.
2 Japan Environment Agency 1976a.

includes the construction or modification of buildings, surface mining, tree cutting and water-level alteration (Japan Environment Agency 1981). Permission for such activities must be obtained from the Director General of the Environment Agency. Private landowners object to these controls much less than in similar situations in the United States and Canada. Lands of special significance in the parks are often purchased by the prefecture with national government assistance.

Quasi-National Parks are also areas of significant national beauty. They are often near an existing National Park and are designated by the Director General of the Environment Agency upon request from the prefectural governor and with the agreement of the Nature Conservation Council. They are put under the administration of the prefecture. In total, there are 51 Quasi-National Parks with an aggregate area of 1,147,201 ha.

Within National and Quasi-National Parks, Special Protection Districts are designated with very restrictive development control. As of March 1981, 12 per cent of National Parks (241,518 ha) and 3.7 per cent of Quasi-National Parks (43,589 ha) were under these very restrictive policies.

Prefectures have the authority to establish parks and most have taken the initiative. These parks also tend to be scenic areas that are large and retain natural values. They are administered by the prefecture and are used for both nature conversation and outdoor recreation. On private lands within these parks controls are established through zoning. In 1981 the total area of the Prefectural Natural Parks was larger than that of the National Parks.

Nature Conservation Areas can be established by either the national government through the Director General of the Environment Agency or any prefectural government. For designation they must fulfil one of the following criteria:

1. A forest or grassland, 800 m or more above sea level and covering 1,000 ha or more. It must contain alpine or semi-alpine plant communities.
2. A forest of 100 ha or more that contains excellent examples of mature trees.
3. An area with unique geographical or geological features such as coast, lake, river or sea area. It must be 10 ha or more in size and contain an excellent natural ecosystem with native plants and animals.

The Nature Conservation Areas are relatively small properties and are found outside the Natural Parks. As of March 1981 there were six areas designated by the national government and 427 designated by the prefectures.

Wilderness Areas are selected from landscapes where the environment is completely natural and unaffected by human activities. These are lands that are owned by one of the governmental levels. They must be 1,000 ha in size or greater and may be found inside a Natural Park. As of March 1981, five Wilderness Areas, totalling 5,631 ha, had been established.

Wildlife Protection Areas are established by the Director General of the

Environment Agency for the shelter and breeding of wildlife. They are utilized in order to prohibit wildlife capture in certain areas, to protect breeding areas of rare species or to manage migratory stopovers. Both national and prefectural governments have set up such areas. By 1976, 2,775 Wildlife Protection Areas covering 2,604,000 ha were in place.

All of the National Parks and wildlife responsibilities are administered by the Nature Conservation Bureau of the Environment Agency. This Agency was established in 1971.

The strong emphasis on scenic beauty in parks is representative of the importance of scenery in Japanese culture. A 1980 survey of domestic tourism found that 49.2 per cent of tourists travelled to enjoy scenic beauty (Japan National Tourist Organization 1981). In a survey of the industrial city of Chiba more than 80 per cent of respondents stated that they travel to places of natural beauty more than once a year (Yoshii 1982).

The importance of the natural environment to Japanese citizens was evident when 90 per cent of respondents to a survey indicated that they felt that the balance of nature is delicate and easily upset and that human beings must live in harmony with nature. Over 60 per cent felt that a citizen has the right to oppose public projects that destroy the environment (Yoshii 1982).

The Prefecture of Wakayama

Introduction
Wakayama is a prefecture located on the main island of Honshu, south-west of Tokyo (Fig. 6.7). The capital is Wakayama. The prefecture is mountainous with many rivers flowing out of the uplands in deep gorges. The coast is beautiful, with white sands, rocky islets and cliffs.

It is 472,300 ha in size with a 1976 population of 1,078,000. It contains seven cities of over 20,000 people with Wakayama the largest at 395,000 (Yano 1978). The population density is intermediate, by Japanese standards, with 228 people per square kilometre. Seven other prefectures have densities well over 600 per sq. km.

The natural environment
The Wakayama prefecture contains between 5 and 10 per cent of its area in natural forests or grasslands compared to 22.8 per cent nationally (Japan Environment Agency 1976b) (Fig. 6.8). Warm, evergreen broadleaf forests occur below 500 m, which is the majority of the area in this prefecture. These contain Japanese chestnut, elm and ash with conifers such as pines, Japanese fir and Japanese cedar. Between 500 and 1400 m a temperate deciduous broadleaf forest is found. It contains Japanese cedar, Japanese cypress, larch, fir, spruce and hemlocks as well as Japanese beech, oaks, maples, ash, chestnut and birches.

105

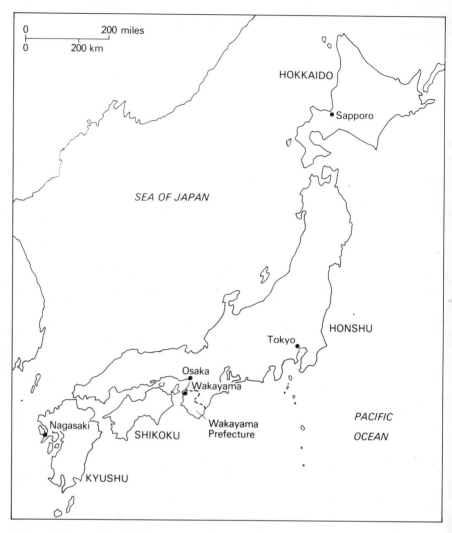

Figure 6.7 Location of Wakayama Prefecture, Honshu Island, Japan
Source: McNelly 1973 (adapted from *National Geographic Magazine Atlas*, pl. 51, Dec. 1960)

Figure 6.8 A Satellite photograph of Southcentral Japan including the Wakayama Prefecture. This ERTS image is a composite of a photograph (northern portion) taken May 2, 1978 and one taken June 15, 1973 (southern portion). The rugged, heavily forested Kii Mountains in the Wakayama Peninsula contrast markedly with heavily developed lowland plains of Osaka. For such a heavily populated island Japan has a remarkable abundance of natural area, mostly forest. The intensive use of the plains and valleys are clearly visible as such land use is light in the photo due to an absence of trees.

Osaka

Osaka
Bay

Gojo

Kinokara River

Wakayama

Arita River

KII MOUNTAINS

Hidaka River

Wakayama
Prefecture

KII CHANNEL

Kamano River

Gubo

Shingu

Tanabe

*PACIFIC
OCEAN*

The area has warm summers with mild dry winters. There are up to 260 frost-free days on the coast with 240 days inland. Total precipitation varies from 120 cm in the west to 250 in the east.

The prefecture is underlain by old sedimentary rocks. It is mountainous with less than 25 per cent of the land having a slope of less than 15 per cent (Trewartha 1965).

Policies

The Wakayama prefecture contains portions of two National Parks, Yoshino-Kumano and Seto-naikai (Fig. 6.9). The first is located along the Pacific shore and inland along a series of rivers and gorges. The latter is located on a series of islands that stretch for 500 km along the beautiful inland sea between Honshu and Shikoku. It has considerable historic interest because it was the main waterway that introduced culture from abroad. Seto-naikai (inland sea of Japan) was designated a National Park in 1934 but at that time it did not include any marine underwater areas. A 1970 amendment to the Natural Parks Act allowed for the protection of underwater resources in National or Quasi-National Parks. By 31 March 1981 a total of 57 marine park areas had been established within 23 parks, including Seto-naikai. But these 57 marine parks totalled only 2,385.3 ha (Japan National Tourist Organization 1981) which is small compared to the total area of terrestrial parks.

The Seto-naikai National Park is a large expanse of water studded with islands. The north-eastern portion is in the Wakayama prefecture. It is really a chain of five bodies of water linked by channels. The numerous islands, beaches and coastal plateaus which command superb views of the water make for a scenic area (National Parks Association of Japan, undated). Combined with the small ports, fishing villages, salt field and farms found on the slopes, the park is part of a rich cultural area (Japan National Tourist Organization 1982). This combination of natural and cultural landscapes within a park is similar to the British concept of the National Park.

There is one Quasi-National Park in Wakayama, Koya-Ryujin. It is a central mountainous area that is well removed from the two national parks.

Wakayama has 10 Prefectural Natural Parks, administered by the prefectural government.

The Prefectural Nature Conservation Areas are designated strictly for conservation purposes. They are small, important nature areas such as shrines, wetlands or stands of a rare species. Wakayama has eight such areas designated.

Prefectural governments have strong and authoritative powers over the uses of private land. Before the postwar constitution private land rights were practically nonexistent. The constitution strengthened the concept of private land ownership but compared to the other countries studied, the government wields much more land-designation power in Japan.

It appears to be difficult to generalize about the role of municipalities in

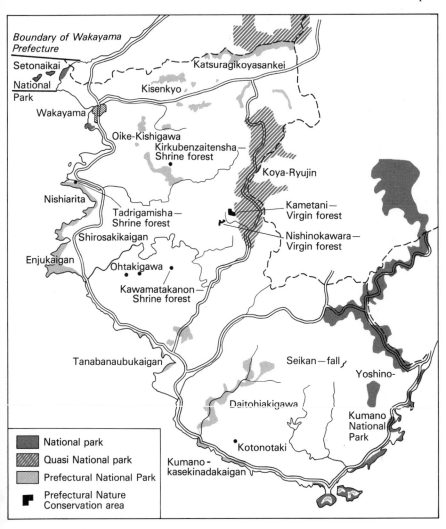

Figure 6.9 Natural Parks of the Wakayama Prefecture of Japan. These natural areas are included in three categories of protected area: National Park, Quasi-National Park and Prefectural Natural Park. The mountainous terrain and relatively low population have resulted in large amounts of natural biological community remaining on the slopes.

environmental conservation in Japan. It depends greatly upon local initiative and resources (Patterson pers. comm.). Some municipalities have extensive parks systems with administrative bodies. Others have very little. Wakayama is average or moderate in this regard. In comparison, Tokyo has established an aggressive environmental agency in order to help alleviate large-scale environmental degradation. In 1972 Tokyo passed the Ordinance Concerning the Conservation and Restoration of Nature in Tokyo. The main idea behind the law was the thinking 'that the conservation of a good natural environment is essential for the protection of the fundamental rights of the citizens' (Tokyo Metropolitan Government 1977, p. 187). The basic elements of the law include:

A mechanism to designate natural areas for conservation;

The establishment of nature protection as the top municipal priority;

A procedure for controlling and limiting future land development so as to protect nature areas;

A general recognition of the need to consider all of nature (air, water, soil, flora and fauna) in planning;

A procedure to restore degraded lands to a natural state;

The establishment of a technical advisory committee (Nature Protection Council) to suggest regulations, research topics and to review development proposals;

The development of a system of volunteer 'green' patrolmen to serve as watchdogs over destructive activities.

Urban ecosystem research in Tokyo has documented the environmental alteration associated with intensive development of this city (Numata 1982). The loss of species, extensive water and air pollution and land alteration has emphasized the importance of local natural areas and thus the development of the conservation law.

Problems and successes

Wakayama appears to be an average prefecture with regard to nature conservation. The lack of a coordinated nation-wide policy requiring the lower governmental levels to have regard for significant natural areas has resulted in a spotty distribution of activity. This is a situation very similar to that found in Canada and the United States, but quite dissimilar from Great Britain, which has such a policy.

Rapid urban development combined with a gradual societal attitude shift away from a respect for nature may be foreboding trends. The excellent national vegetation data base gives environmental managers a solid basis on which to develop policy at the local level, if they so desire.

The success of society in protecting natural areas in the past is commendable. The role of the municipal governments in this action appears to be only one factor and possibly a minor one.

Conclusions

The national and prefectural governments have the authority designating conservation areas, irrespective of land ownership. The land need not be purchased before designation (Ikenouye pers. comm.). Such designation is now moving forward at both levels, with considerable success. At present 427 areas have been designated as Prefectural Nature Conservation Areas (total area 76,334 ha) and 293 areas as Prefectural Natural Parks (2,045,234 ha).

The long-standing respect shown to nature by the citizen and the tradition of obeying government decree have both contributed to the success of the various programmes. In terms of area, the 20.99 per cent of the country (Table 6.1) in one of the classes of protected areas is quite remarkable.

City development continues to occur but the Ministry of Construction, which enforces the city planning laws, and the Environment Agency negotiate the designation of areas to be developed or protected.

Japan has only a few decades of experience with the new structure of government. The divisions of power are still being worked out with overlap and shared responsibilities being common. Environmental conservation appears to have made a strong foothold in the decision-making institutions.

Canada

Introduction

Canada is a large country of 9,976,128 sq. km with a relatively small population of 24.5 million people in 1982. It is also a young country with approximately 200 years of development since the European settlement and 115 years since confederation and relative independence from Great Britain.

The urban and agricultural development is almost totally concentrated along the southern edge of the country close to the border with the United States. In this corridor of development the land-use change within the last 150 years has been dramatic. The deciduous forests in the east and coniferous forests in the west on the deep soils have largely been cleared for agriculture. The grassland soils in the central parts of the country have been ploughed and used for grain production. In the hinterland forests very few areas of virgin timber remain, since the vast majority of the forests have been felled at some time in the past.

Since the time of the Second World War the urban development has been dramatic, with very extensive urban growth in southern Ontario, southwestern British Columbia and south-western Quebec. Nevertheless, the country still retains some of the largest and most natural wilderness areas in the world. The extensive National Park system of the federal government and the Provincial Park systems of each of the 10 provinces protect many of these areas. Within the developed areas, fragments of the original ecosystems still remain, many with only a minor degree of human-caused alteration. This case study concentrates on the initiative of one municipal jurisdiction regarding the inventory, protection and management of these relict landscapes.

Institutional environment

Canada is a federated country composed of ten provinces and two territories. The provinces have authority over natural resources, municipal institutions and property rights which means that local land-use regulations and day-to-day operations are influenced very little by the national government. The territories contain the sparsely populated northern half of the country and are under the direct influence of the federal government.

Canada has an extensive system of 28 National Parks that covers 12,965,580 ha (32,037,948 acres) with a 1979–80 visitation of 20.7 million people (Parks Canada 1981). The basic purpose of these parks is to preserve large portions of the environment in as natural a state as possible (Parks Canada 1979). Development is restricted to that necessary for visitor use and park management, with the exception of a few townsites that occur in the oldest parks. Ontario has four National Parks with one more being proposed (Eagles *et al.* 1981). The existing parks are 191,160 ha (472,356 acres) in size with a 1979–80 visitation of 812,510 people (Parks Canada 1981).

Ontario has a large system of 132 Provincial Parks that cover 4.2 million hectares (10.4 m. acres) of land. These parks vary in purpose from wilderness and nature reserve (Ministry of Natural Resources 1981) through to intensive recreational development. The government is working towards the establishment of a system of parks that protects representative samples of each ecosystem type that occurs in the Province, from Carolinean forest in the south to arctic tundra in the north (Beechey and Davidson 1980).

Conservation Authorities are independent government authorities that are established according to the limits of the various watersheds that occur in the settled parts of the province. They are established under the authority of Ontario provincial law. Their funding comes from both land tax and provincial government grants. Conservation Authorities have two major responsibilities, water management and urban outdoor recreation. All 39 Conservation Authorities are heavily involved in the purchase and management of local natural areas. By 1977 they had opened 303 local parks, called Conservation Areas, that covered 37 000 ha (91,427 acres). Almost twice this area was held in a natural state without any recreational facility development (Eagles 1979).

All provinces have some type of Planning Act which lays down the rules for the operation of a legal recognized municipal land-use regulation system. In each municipality this system has two major components: an overall policy plan or Official Plan and a secondary set of detailed zoning by-laws that implement the general policies.

The operation of the municipalities themselves is governed by two pieces of provincial legislation, the law which established the municipality and an omnibus Municipal Act which governs day-to-day municipal operation and decision making. Over time a complex assortment of municipalities has been created by provincial statute including villages, towns, cities, townships, counties, districts and the newest form, urban-centred regions. The local municipalities are on the front line of land-use planning and make the important land allocation decisions concerning all private land. However, most provinces retain some form of veto that can be used to vary or overrule muncipal decisions.

Before 1970, in both the Province of Ontario and the rest of Canada, the subject of nature conservation was not normally part of the policy concern of local municipal planning departments. In the early 1970s several studies were completed that pointed out the possibilities of municipalities becoming involved in the protection of local natural areas. Chanasyk (1970) in the Haldimand-Norfolk Region utilized environmental planning concepts, based upon considerable historical ecology, to develop a landscape analysis. Dorney and George (1970) detailed areas worthy of long-term protection in the County of Waterloo. The Ottawa Field Naturalists' Club (1970) outlined to the Ottawa-Carleton Region natural areas that should be protected in the new Official Plan under preparation.

These initiatives coincided with the Province of Ontario starting to reorganize County governments into Regional governments, along the model of the earlier Metropolitan Toronto Regional government. While planning in Ontario is not a compulsory function of municipal governments, in the case of Regions the enabling legislation dictated that Official Plans must be created and time limits set for their adoption. Also, all Official Plans and zoning by-laws of the local municipalities, cities, towns and townships must be brought into conformity with the Regional Official Plan.

This new legislation set the stage for widespread initiatives in planning. One of these was the introduction of environmental management principles, generally, and Environmentally Sensitive Area policies, specifically, into the developing plans. The planners and the ecological and environmental advisory committee of the Region of Waterloo took the earlier ideas and developed them into a workable policy framework. They used the words Environmentally Sensitive Area for the first time. They developed criteria for the definition of these areas. They supervised a Region-wide inventory that delineated areas that fit the criteria. They developed a policy implementation framework using environmental impact assessments and reviews of the technical advisory committee. Faculty and students of the three local universities, Waterloo, Guelph and Wilfrid Laurier were heavily involved in giving advice and undertaking inventories. The resultant Official Plan was a considerable advance in the field (Region of Waterloo 1976). This work set the stage for the further development by the Region of Halton (Eagles 1979).

The protection of a representative number of natural ecosystem types will require a coordinated system approach at a variety of scales and by a variety of government levels, as was outlined in Chapter 4. Francis (1978) has discussed the development of such a system in southern Ontario. The national government would concentrate on protecting large, nationally-

113

significant blocks of land in National Parks. The provincial government would protect a set of Provincial Parks that contain provincially-significant ecosystems. Local municipalities and Conservation Authorities could use their resources to identify and manage local Environmentally Sensitive Areas through a variety of arrangements. Such an overall system approach is starting to take shape in Ontario.

The Regional Municipality of Halton, Ontario

Introduction

The Regional Municipality of Halton is located in south-central Ontario along the northern shore of Lake Ontario (Fig. 6.10). It is a restructured County with a powerful council composed of local elected councillors who are appointed to the upper-tier body by the local municipal councils. This second-tier municipal structure was created by the Provincial Government

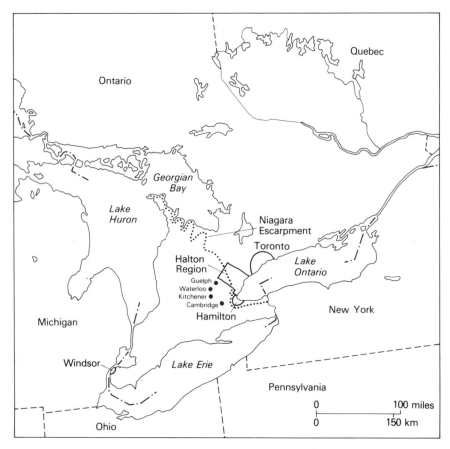

Figure 6.10 Location of Halton Region, Ontario, Canada

to provide a local political body that could handle the pressures of rapid economic and urban growth. In the case of Halton each of the four local cities or towns appoints councillors to the Regional council proportional to the local population. The county covers 95,832 ha and has a population of 225,000. It is a relatively wealthy area with a large number of residences owned by influential businessmen and professionals who work in the industrial city of Hamilton immediately to the south-west and the major financial centre of Toronto to the east.

The creation of the restructured Regions out of the earlier Counties has been controversial, with many individuals and local municipalities opposed to the loss of decision-making powers to the new powerful body. Nevertheless, the restructured Counties, now called Regions, have remained in place through their first 10 years and it looks at if they will remain. Each Region was given the statutory obligation to develop and implement a new region-wide Official Plan. This plan does not show individual properties or detailed boundaries but is a policy plan that must deal with region-wide issues on a general level. The local municipalities have the job of developing a detailed Official Plan and the implementing zoning by-laws within the structure imposed by the Regional Plan.

Once a Regional Plan is approved by the Minister of Housing and Municipal Affairs for the Ontario Provincial Government, all local municipal plans must be brought into conformity. This process is now under way. In addition, the lower-level municipal government must redraft their zoning by-laws in accordance with the new plans.

The natural environment
This portion of Ontario was originally covered by a forest composed of deciduous trees including maple, ash, oak and beech, at the time of land settlement around 1800. Over the next 60 years the majority of these forests were felled and the land cleared for agricultural purposes. Two cities, Burlington and Oakville, slowly grew and developed on the shores of Lake Ontario. After 1945 the cities grew very rapidly.

The physical character of Halton is dominated by a distinctive limestone escarpment that cuts diagonally across the Region. This 100 m high cliff and its associated valleys and slopes is unsuitable for agriculture and as a result large areas of forest still remain in its vicinity. At present the remaining natural ecosystems are found along the Niagara Escarpment, in deep river valleys, in undrained wetlands or in farmer's woodlots. The rest of the area is covered by agricultural fields, urban development or transportation facilities (Fig. 6.11).

Halton has one of the highest percentages of forest of any Region or County in southern Ontario. Around 20 per cent of its area is relatively natural. This figure is much more than most of the agricultural counties, which vary between 2 and 8 per cent forest.

Figure 6.11 A Satellite Photograph of Southern Ontario including the Municipality (County) of Halton.   Southern Ontario is one of the most heavily developed areas in Canada with large cities, heavy industry and active agriculture. This ERTS image taken in June 19, 1979 clearly shows that many natural areas, as shown by blotches of dark forest, still exist. The influence of the Niagara Escarpment and the rugged lands north and west of this ridge is evidenced by a general dark band of forested land, part of which is in Halton. The ESA program in Ontario is an attempt by many individuals and institutions to develop planning and management policies for the long-term protection of the remaining significant natural areas. Most of the ESA's shown in Figure 6.13 are visible in this satellite photograph.

The weather can be typified as being hot in the summer, with frequent but short showers, and cold in the winter, with snow. During July the daily highs go above 25 degrees C, while in January they hover around –2 degrees C. The total yearly precipitation averages 78 cm. Along Lake Ontario 160 frost-free days occur, while inland 140 days can be expected (Crowe *et al.* 1977).

Figure 6.12 illustrates the Environmentally Sensitive Areas that fulfil the criteria discussed in Chapter 4. The effects of the escarpment and river

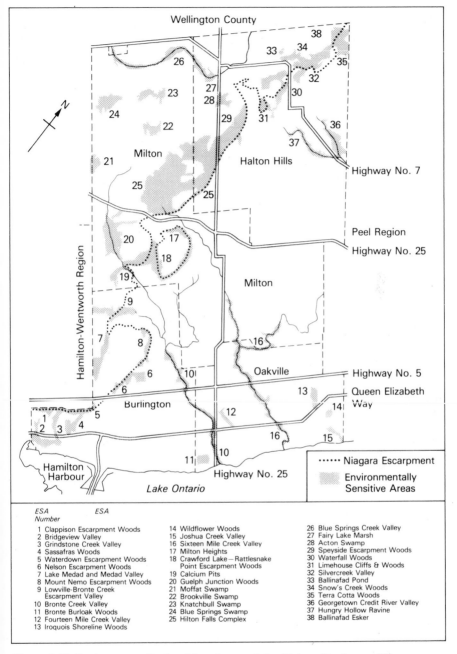

Wellington County

38
33 34
26 35
32
23 27 30
28
24 29 31
22 36
37
21 Milton Halton Hills
25 Highway No. 7
25
Peel Region
20 17 Highway No. 25
18
19
Milton
9

7 8
6 16
6 10 Oakville Highway No. 5
6 13 Queen Elizabeth
Burlington 14 Way
1 5 12
2 3 4
16 15
11 10
Hamilton 11 ····· Niagara Escarpment
Harbour Highway No. 25 Environmentally
Lake Ontario Sensitive Areas

Hamilton-Wentworth Region

ESA Number	ESA	
1 Clappison Escarpment Woods	14 Wildflower Woods	26 Blue Springs Creek Valley
2 Bridgeview Valley	15 Joshua Creek Valley	27 Fairy Lake Marsh
3 Grindstone Creek Valley	16 Sixteen Mile Creek Valley	28 Acton Swamp
4 Sassafras Woods	17 Milton Heights	29 Speyside Escarpment Woods
5 Waterdown Escarpment Woods	18 Crawford Lake – Rattlesnake	30 Waterfall Woods
6 Nelson Escarpment Woods	Point Escarpment Woods	31 Limehouse Cliffs & Woods
7 Lake Medad and Medad Valley	19 Calcium Pits	32 Silvercreek Valley
8 Mount Nemo Escarpment Woods	20 Guelph Junction Woods	33 Ballinafad Pond
9 Lowville-Bronte Creek	21 Moffat Swamp	34 Snow's Creek Woods
Escarpment Valley	22 Brookville Swamp	35 Terra Cotta Woods
10 Bronte Creek Valley	23 Knatchbull Swamp	36 Georgetown Credit River Valley
11 Bronte Burloak Woods	24 Blue Springs Swamp	37 Hungry Hollow Ravine
12 Fourteen Mile Creek Valley	25 Hilton Falls Complex	38 Ballinafad Esker
13 Iroquois Shoreline Woods		

Figure 6.12 Environmentally Sensitive Areas of the Halton Region.   These significant natural areas are forests that have survived the land clearance for agricultural and urban development. The rocky Niagara Escarpment and many river valleys were unsuitable for development and therefore were allowed to remain in forest in the past.
Source: Region of Halton 1978

117

valleys in limiting land clearance are obvious. The absence of significant wetland ecosystems along the lakeshore is largely due to the nature of the shore, a steep, linear bluff constantly exposed to the open lake and the presence of urban development. The inventory and delineation of the ESAs were supervised by a local environmental advisory committee with the assistance of provincial government grants for inventory assistance (Tant *et al.* 1977; Region of Halton 1978; Armour *et al.* 1979; *Ecologistics* 1979; Paton and Sharp 1979; Jakab *et al.* 1980; Sutherland 1981).

Policies

No National Parks occur in Halton but Bronte Creek Provincial Park was opened in 1973. This 641 ha (1,920 acres) recreation-class park contains a deep, forested river valley that runs through a flat tableland with numerous fields and farms. The river valley forests with their plant and animal populations fulfil several ESA criteria. The park is protecting these areas in the approved Master Plan (Ministry of Natural Resources 1972).

The Halton, Hamilton and Credit Conservation Authorities each have jurisdiction over a portion of the County. Conservation Authorities under Ontario Law are independent government bodies with resource management responsibilities, and most specifically deal with water management and near-urban Parks. Each authority has extensive land-holdings, including a number of ESAs. For example, Mountsberg Wildlife area is a large wetland and forest complex managed by the Halton Authority. In addition portions of the Niagara Escarpment and many small marsh and forested wetlands are owned and managed by the Authorities. In total, the three Conservation Authorities own approximately 2,400 ha (5,930 acres) of ESAs in Halton. On a portion of this area 13 Conservation Areas (Parks) have been developed (Hall and Menyes pers. comm.). But even with the holdings by the province and the three Authorities, the majority of the ESAs are in private ownership.

The Regional Municipality of Halton has an Official Plan approved by the regional council and the provincial government, with the exception of certain sections referred to the Ontario Municipal Board for a hearing. It is a plan with legal force.

The plan has typical policies such as those dealing with housing, population and economic development. It also contains a large number of resource management policies under categories such as hazard lands, waterfront, open space, agriculture, forestry, mineral resources, energy, solid waste management, parkway belt, Niagara Escarpment (Fig. 6.13) and Environmentally Sensitive Areas.

One of the goals of the plan under the heading of Growth and Settlement states that the Region of Halton (1980, p. 11) wishes:

To manage growth in accordance with the Region's desire to improve and maintain regional unity, retain local community identity and maintain a high quality natural environment.

Figure 6.13 Photograph of Niagara Escarpment. The flat clay plains of lowland Halton County contain a variety of agricultural landscapes that contrast with rugged forest lands above the Niagara Escarpment. The cliffs and their associated deciduous forests can be seen on the horizon.
Source: Niagara Escarpment Commission 1979

Another goal under the heading of Environmental Protection States that the Region desires to 'protect environmentally significant areas of the regional landscape' (p. 13). while specific plan objectives desire (p. 14):

> To identify, protect and preserve lands of sensitive environmental balance, including: headwater control and aquifer recharge areas, wetlands, fish and wildlife habitats, streams and river valleys, areas of unique biological features, areas of outstanding scenic beauty.
>
> To define hazard lands for the protection of life and property.
>
> To permit development only in environmentally suitable areas.

The effort to maintain this environmental quality is reflected in corresponding policies through the plan that attempt to conserve existing forest cover, protect ecological lands from surface mining, protect the Niagara Escarpment and ensure indepth environmental impact assessments of large development projects. Regarding Environmentally Sensitive Areas it is the policy of the Region to:

1. Restrict alteration of the physical and/or biological features of 38 Environmentally Sensitive Areas (E.S.A.'s).

2. Require, where the physical and/or biological features of an E.S.A. may become altered, that an Environmental Impact Assessment (E.I.A.) be carried out by the proponent, except where specifically exempted elsewhere in the Plan.
3. Encourage development which may alter the physical and/or biological features of E.S.A.'s to locate outside E.S.A.'s.
4. Require that public works that may alter such features be subject to an E.I.A.
5. Define guidelines for Environmental Impact Assessments, with the assistance of appropriate Provincial agencies.
6. Encourage Conservation Authorities and other appropriate public agencies to acquire all or part of E.S.A.'s as they become available. However E.S.A. identification does not imply that such area will be purchased by a public agency nor that it is open for public use.
7. Require local by-laws and encourage Conservation Authority and Provincial regulations implementing this Plan to provide controls for the protection of E.S.A.'s.
8. Require local Official Plans to indicate E.S.A.'s on the understanding that precise boundaries will be established through E.I.A.
9. Establish means of protection where an E.S.A. is endangered by a proposed nearby change in land use.
10. Establish procedures for handling development applications which could alter the physical and/or biological features of an E.S.A. These include a specific requirement for conducting an E.I.A.
11. Support the Area Municipalities in defending E.S.A. policies through provision of available data and comments on E.I.A.'s.
12. Require that the alteration of any condition or land use of an E.S.A. which may affect the features for which it was identified be subject to the approval of the appropriate authority, based on site plans submitted by, and agreements entered into with, the proponent.
13. Consider entering into agreements with E.S.A. landowners to ensure protection of E.S.A.'s.
14. (a) Monitor and review development proposals that are subject to E.S.A. policies or other regulations with respect to E.S.A.'s through the Halton Region Ecological and Environmental Advisory Committee (E.E.A.C.).
(b) Encourage environmental research and the monitoring of cumulative change within E.S.A.'s.
15. Require that E.E.A.C. review each E.I.A. provided under this Plan, and make recommendations to the appropriate body, through the Planning Committee, as part of the Development Control process.

16. Require application of these policies uniformly for all land uses excluding such structures and their use as have been approved within E.S.A.'s prior to the adoption of this Plan.
17. Ensure that the land Division Committee reject or approve all severances where E.S.A. features may become altered, on the basis of E.E.A.C. and Regional Staff comments, with any approvals to be subject to conditions and or agreements designed to protect the E.S.A. features. E.I.A.'s will not, however, be required for such applications. (Region of Halton, 1980, pp. 55, 56, 57).

In addition the Province of Ontario has established a special purpose body, the Niagara Escarpment Commission, to develop policies for the conservation and management of the ecologically and aesthetically valuable Niagara Escarpment. The proposed plan for this area has been the subject of hearings for several years and its ultimate form is as yet unclear (Niagara Escarpment Commission 1979). This plan has a similar intent to the ESA policies of the region, the protection of ecologically sensitive lands.

Problems and successes
The Halton Plan and the associated inventories, publications, advisory committee and public profile illustrate a recent fundamental advance in local environmental management. The residents of the Region through their elected representatives are stating that the ESAs are important and are worthy of protection. The inclusion in the plan of ESA policies as well as other more all-encompassing environmental policies is a recognition that municipal government decisions do have an important role to play in the management of the local environment.

Some of the existing development interests in the community have not looked favourably upon the attempt to limit negative environmental impact in selected areas. The aggregate extraction industry in particular has been aggressive in its opposition because of its interest in surface mining on large portions of the Niagara Escarpment. In this case the conflict can be described in relatively black and white terms because the mining will result in the complete removal of the surface ecosystem. The economic value of the limestone bedrock is such that the corporations wishing to mine are unwilling to agree to any limitation on extraction. The companies have taken the Regional government to court on the premise that the municipalities do not have the right to implement environmental policies of this type. The case is now (1983) being heard and the decision will be important for future activities. Swaigen (1979) has discussed the legal issues surrounding the conflict between private ownership rights and public environment rights with regard to conservation planning, such as is taking place in Halton.

Conclusions

The Halton Plan is only one example of several dozen similar initiatives undertaken in Canada's municipalities (Eagles 1981). The protective policies are strongest in those areas that have undergone rapid development in the last few decades. The public, the politicians and the planners appear willing to attempt ESA protection and management where the examples of past natural destruction are immediately obvious. The old truth that scarcity breeds value also appears to work here. Therefore the majority of the ESA initiatives are found in the urbanizing portions of the country.

The rural municipalities often see little value in worrying about something that is all around them. Correspondingly, the attitudes of rural people are such that the natural environment is often viewed as an obstacle to progress and not as a resource to protect. This view has its roots in the European immigrant's idea that the North American wilderness must be conquered and civilized.

In Canada, the development pressure on the local natural areas is probably less than in any of the four countries discussed in this chapter. It is a large country with a relatively small population. The policies appear to be based on a general, but still developing, consensus that the Canadian natural environment is a heritage worthy of consideration. The level of consideration varies from complete protection in many federal and provincial parks and reserves to a general attempt at conservation of important areas on private land in local municipalities.

The pressures continue for the conversion of natural ecosystems and farmland into other uses that produce economic return for certain segments of the population. The surface mining, intensive forestry and agricultural, industrial and urban development interests will continue to put severe pressure on the remaining natural areas. The important element about the Canadian experience is that the protection of important natural areas is now being given consideration along with the economic, social and political factors that have largely determined municipal land use planning in the past.

United States

Introduction

The United States is a large country of 9,363,353 sq. km. and over 226,500,000 people in 1980. It has had over 200 years of development since independence from Britain. Each of the 50 states has had a unique historical development so that the country has a complete set of political institutions at the local level.

The development of the country has involved one of the most dramatic landscape changes known to mankind. In the last 300 years, large areas of forests, prairies and deserts were converted to agricultural or urban landscapes. The indigenous peoples were either moved aside or eliminated by the tide of European invasion. Along with these alterations a conservation ethic began to develop and spread. One visible ramification of this approach has been the protection of areas of virgin countryside in a system of magnificent National Parks, National Monuments, Wildlife Refuges and State Parks. The world's first National Park was created at Yellowstone in 1873 and since that time the concept has spread world-wide.

Most of the 50 states maintain state park systems that contribute significantly to the protection of significant landscapes. In addition, the Endangered Species Act is the most advanced legislation of its type in the world. It has resulted in the delineation and protection of many endangered species.

Institutional environment

The United States is a federated country composed of 50 states and a number of protectorates. States have authority over municipalities which results in little direct interaction between the national and local governments. The vast majority of the settled areas have incorporated local municipalities with the County being a standard, ubiquitous institution.

Most municipalities maintain a land-use planning function, with various degrees of emphasis. Some concentrate only on developing and operating a zoning ordinance while others develop comprehensive policy plans as well. Usually the state governments do not play a major approval role for municipal plans, with the exception of specific policy areas where special subsidies are provided. This is fundamentally different from Canada and Great Britain where the provincial and national governments, respectively, are heavily involved in guiding and approving municipal plans.

The fifth amendment of the United States constitution states that 'private property (shall not) be taken without just compensation'. The courts have interpreted certain land-use regulations to constitute a 'taking' of private property. If government physically invades the land it is under the eminent domain power; if it influences the land otherwise it is an exercise of the police power. A difficulty arises in the preservation of open space by use of the police power because there is a lack of objective standards for determining whether a use restriction is reasonable. In a variety of cases, US courts have ruled as invalid zoning ordinances restricting land use for flood storage, parking lots, school, recreation, open space, green-belt, and park purposes. Similarly, some subdivision regulations have been invalidated (Rose 1974; Bosselman 1975).

In 1972 the Supreme Court stated in *Just* v. *Marinette County* in Wisconsin that:

(An) owner of land has no absolute and unlimited right to change the essential character of his land so as to use it for a purpose for which it was unsuited in its natural state and which injures the rights of others (as quoted in DiResta 1982, p. 493).

The 1980 case of *Agins* v. *City of Tiburon* (100 *Supreme Court Reporter* 2138) has the potential of further reinterpreting the issues of downzoning and taking. The Supreme Court unanimously agreed that the zoning ordinances of Tiburon that restricted development to between one and five residences on 5 acres (2 ha) of unimproved land did not constitute a taking. The court stated that the zoning ordinance benefited both the landowner and the city by 'assuring careful and orderly development of residential property'. The judgement implied that the city's concerns of preserving the environment and open space planning were valid concerns and within their jurisdiction (Eagles 1981). Rohrs (1981) has stated that *Agins* gives zoning authorities an almost unlimited power in using zoning to influence development density and protect open space. These authorities will be able to protect open space without buying it as long as some remaining reasonable economic use is allowed: residential use is one such remnant use. A municipality or state can be sure of having the power of protecting open space for viewing, but it cannot guarantee physical access without paying the owner.

In 1981 the Florida Supreme Court in the case of *Graham* v. *Estuary Properties* ruled that:

> once there is sufficient evidence of an adverse impact, it is neither unconstitutional nor unreasonable to require the developer to prove that the proposed curative measures will be adequate (as quoted by DiResta 1982, p. 492).

The court had upheld the denial of permission to destroy 1,800 acres (728 ha) of mangroves for a proposed residential development. It was ruled that the wetland loss would constitute a public harm as the mangrove swamps were considered to be areas of critical state concern (DiResta 1982).

Over time the case law appears to have established the rule that governments can limit development on land, as long as some economic use remains. Large lots, such as the five-acre (2 ha) minimum lot size in a designated rural zone in Montgomery County, are an acceptable allowable use. Recently, natural environment concerns are being more and more recognized as being valid bases for development prohibition. This is becoming similar to the situation in Britain and Canada where municipalities have the legal authority to restrict all building on private land, although in these countries the political ramifications may still be negative if such a restriction is attempted.

The 'taking' issue is one that haunts all land-use restriction in the US. It has resulted in widespread and scattered urban development. In areas with a poorly developing municipal planning framework, development occurs in quite a patchwork pattern as private ownership is given more weight than site suitability, municipal service cost or community consensus.

In an effort to preserve farmland and Environmentally Sensitive Areas, some jurisdictions are allowing the sale and transfer of development rights (TDR) from one parcel to another. The 'right' to develop land is a codified principle resulting from the fifth amendment. In Montgomery County, agricultural reserve areas have been designated as development rights sending areas. Correspondingly, other areas near urban developments are designated as development rights receiving areas. Owners in the sending area are allowed only one lot per 10 ha but can sell these 'rights' to develop and they can be transferred to receiving areas. Here the legally allowed density can be increased with the transferred development rights (Coleman and Perrine 1982).

This complex and novel TDR concept has developed as a result of the legal framework in the United States. It may prove to be helpful in saving Environmentally Sensitive Areas from the disturbance that would result if every landowner in such an area decided to build on his property.

The difficulty of enforcing development restrictions has caused many officials to consider that environmental protection of common property land resources is best done by government land purchase (Kershow 1975).

The County of Montgomery, Maryland

Introduction

Montgomery County is located in Maryland adjacent to Washington DC in the Washington-Baltimore Corridor (Fig. 6.14). The county is 131,000 ha in size with a population of 590,000 in 1979. The urban areas are concentrated in the southern corner of the county adjacent to Washington. Elsewhere, much of the land is rural in character with amounts of forest, valley and farmland. Rapid urbanization took place in the 1960s and 1970s. It has been predicted that by 1998 the population will have grown to 680,000, an increase of 15 per cent (Maryland-National Capital Park and Planning Commission 1976; Montgomery County Planning Board 1979). Through the 1960s approximately half of the country's farmland changed to non-farm ownership. At least 50 per cent of the workforce commutes to employment in Washington but this percentage is decreasing as jobs are developed in the county (Coleman and Perrine 1982).

Montgomery and Prince George's Counties surround Washington DC on the Maryland side. This intimate contact with the nation's capital has resulted in pressure for extensive land development and the constituent need for coordinated and long-term land-use planning. The state of Maryland passed enabling legislation to establish a two-county planning body – the Maryland-National Capital Park and Planning Commission. This Commission is a planning authority and in addition administers a 10,000 ha (25,000 acre) park system which it owns. The Commission is composed of 10 members, five from each county, and is appointed by the county governments. Each five-member group forms a planning board for that county. Most day-to-day business is handled by the planning boards but all major decisions, such as plan adoption, are made by the full commission (Tustian pers. comm.).

The Commission is also preparing a series of watershed plans for each of the drainage basins. These plans work out the hydrological regime for the

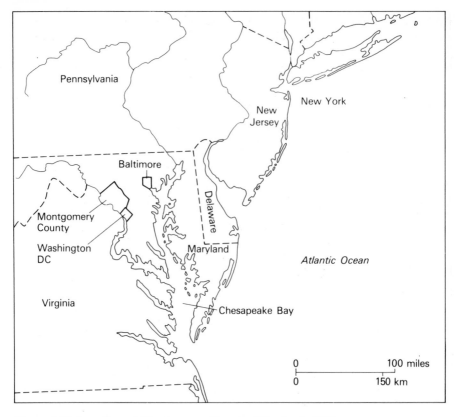

Figure 6.14 Location of Montgomery County, Maryland, USA

basin, delimit the 100-year flood plain and make recommendations on water quality.

The county has extensive parkland owned and managed by a number of governments including the local municipalities, the Maryland-National Capital Park and Planning commission, the state and the federal government. The county has benefited from its location in that several state and national programmes have encouraged park purchase and development, including federal subsidies for stream valley acquisition in the Washington area (Montgomery County Planning Board 1978). Future plans call for a considerable amount of acquisition for recreation, conservation and historic preservation purposes.

The natural environment
Montgomery County is inland, located midway between the Atlantic ocean and the Appalachian mountains (Fig. 6.15). It lies in parts of three physiographic provinces. The gently undulating, low coastal plain touches the eastern edge of the County. Over 75 per cent of the area is located in Piedmont Province, a belt of rolling hills underlain by crystalline metamorphic

Figure 6.15 A Satellite Photograph of Maryland including Montgomery County. This ERTS image, taken on June 30, 1978, shows the distribution of remnant forested lands quite clearly. The forests show as dark areas while urban areas and heavily cultivated areas are light in colour. Even in such an urbanized corridor as that between Washington and Baltimore significant natural areas remain, often associated with steep slopes and river valleys. For example, the slopes of the Potomac River and adjacent tributaries contain extensive amounts of forest.

rocks. In the western corner is the Triassic lowland, a gently rolling plain broken by long low ridges. Across the county from south-east to north-west, elevation increases from just above sea level to up to 275 m (Metropolitan Washington Council of Governments 1968). Approximately 40 per cent of the county has slopes of over 10 per cent with half of this over 20 per cent (Thompson *et al.* 1977).

It is a rolling pastoral landscape with numbers of streams draining to the

Potomac river along the southern boundary (Fig. 6.16). The river valleys often contain bottomland forests on the floodplains and upland woods along the steeper slopes. Wetlands of many types occur including floodplain forests, ponds, marshes, sedge meadows and creeks. The swamp forests contain sycamore, ash and willow trees. Mature, upland forests can still be found in old farm woodlots and along steep slopes where cutting and tilling is difficult. These drier forests are dominated by a diverse set of deciduous hardwoods including red, black, chestnut, scarlet and white oaks as well as gum, beech, maple, pignut and shagbark hickory (Dietmann and Giraldi 1974).

The majority of the tillable lands have been cleared for agriculture. Many of these fields have now been abandoned and are regrowing with a mixture of scrub pine and oak as well as brambles and bushes.

Montgomery County's climate can be described as having hot summers and cool winters. The July daily temperature high averages 24 degrees C while in January it averages 1 degree C. The county has approximately 190 frost-free days, which is lower than the 220 days for shoreline areas along Chesapeake Bay to the east. The total precipitation is slightly over 100 cm per year, of which only 5 cm is snow (Thompson *et al.* 1977).

Rapid urban and estate home development has altered large areas of the agricultural and forested lands. In total, Maryland has 46 per cent of its land

Figure 6.16 Photograph of Montgomery County.   Montgomery County has a diverse topography with low hills, fields, rivers, small lakes and urban development. Over 11,800 ha (26,000 acres) of natural landscape is owned by the Maryland-National Capital Park and Planning Commission.
Source: Maryland-National Capital Park and Planning Commission 1976

surface in forest while Montgomery County has just over 30 per cent forested (Thompson *et al.* 1977).

Policies

As early as 1968 the Washington Metropolitan Council of Governments asked: how can prime agricultural lands, scenic slopes and vistas, and unique plant and wildlife habitats be preserved, in view of traditional urban land economics and land use competition? Concurrently, it proposed that 'unique and economically significant plant and wildlife habitats' be identified and described.

The General Plan for Montgomery County was approved by the Maryland-National Capital Park and Planning Commission in 1969 (Montgomery County Planning Board 1969). It was an update of an earlier 1964 plan. The plan, termed the Wedges and Corridors Plan, provides county-wide policies. At a lower scale to this, Master Plans have been produced for selected areas of the County. These plans are detailed with specific land-use recommendations, facility locations and zoning categories. Intensively developed areas within a Master plan, such as a Central Business District, may have a special sector plan. Zoning ordinances provide the details of the plans. All plans must be approved by the Montgomery County Council and then by the Commission. Table 6.2 shows that these levels of planning found in Montgomery County are almost identical to those occurring in the Region of Halton in Canada. This should not be surprising, since both countries adopted the county political unit from Britain.

The General Plan for Montgomery County has a short policy statement that addresses the protection of ESAs directly. One conservation goal is to:

Table 6.2 A comparison between the local government planning levels in Ontario and Maryland

Canada Ontario Halton Region	United States Maryland Montgomery County	Function
Regional Plan (1978)	General Plan (1969)	County-wide policies
City or town Official Plan	Master Plan	Specific plans for areas of county, with land-use recommendation, facility locations
Secondary Plan	Sector Plan	Detailed plans for communities, business districts or unit areas
Subdivision Plan	Subdivision Plan	Design for urban development
Restricted Area By-law	Zoning Ordinance	Zoning by-law for the specific determination of allowable land uses

'Conserve valuable natural and historic areas for the benefit of present and future generations' (p. 23)

Objectives under this goal desire to:

'Preserve unique and representative biological areas and other features' (p. 24):

'Promote a program for the identification and preservation of important natural areas' (p. 24).

The details of the implementation of these goals and objectives are found scattered throughout the plan. The prohibition or restriction of land uses is not mentioned because, as the County Planning Director stated, 'the taking issue here is a very real one' (Tustian pers. comm.). The implementation of these policies has been accomplished by the careful weaving of complementary policies throughout the plan. For example, it is the policy of the Montgomery County to:

'Protect stream valley corridors to reduce flooding, pollution, and sedimentation and to preserve ecological features' (p. 23).

'Provide for development in urban and suburban areas that retains ecological features and is compatible with good conservation practices' (p. 24).

'Incorporate natural features into existing urban areas to provide the urban dweller with a sense of nature and diversity' (p. 24).

'Provide an aesthetic and healthful environment for present and future generations' (p. 25).

'Preserve natural beauty by providing the proper relationship between population density and open areas' (p. 12).

'Give priority consideration to unique natural areas in parkland and open space acquisition areas' (p. 17).

'Acquire stream valley parks' (p. 18).

'Manage the park system on the basis of sound conservation principles and practices, recognizing the ecological interdependencies of people, flora and fauna, soils and waters' (p. 18).

These policies give a clear statement of the county's desire to conserve and protect natural areas. The major tools for implementation include land acquisition, careful urban design and the direction of development into areas considered suitable. The provision of services, such as sewers, water mains and transportation facilities is an important determinant of the location and speed of development. This has been recognized in the plan policies which state that the county will:

'Make public investments in community facilities in the most efficient manner to insure compact, orderly urban development and maximum service' (p. 15), and

'Provide water and sewerage works in areas where development is desirable' (p. 25).

In other words, the utilities will be kept away from unique and representative ecological areas, and thus reduce the constituent development pressure. The land acquisition has concentrated on the forested river valleys due to a policy decision to purchase 'all of the stream valley land within the county' (Tustian pers. comm.). Some of the valley lands purchase has been by federal and State Park agencies.

The county has not undertaken an inventory of all of the areas that would be considered to be ESAs in Canada and SSSIs in Britain. In the US the words ESA tend to refer to a wide range of lands with cultural, hazardous or ecological significance.

Problems and successes
The Montgomery County General Plan has a sophisticated environmental component, especially so considering that it was developed and approved in the 1960s. The environmental management policies are interwoven throughout the policy plan. Urban development has been encouraged to locate outside important environmental sites.

The taking issue limits the ability of the municipal planning authorities to designate land with environmental features for low levels of development. The courts have dictated that some economic return from the land must be allowed, which usually translates into some form of residential housing. Montgomery County has an agricultural land preservation policy which allows residential urban development at a minimum lot size of 10 ha (25 acres). This appears to be the maximum restriction that the County found to be acceptable. In addition, the owners have the ability to transfer development rights for monetary compensation.

No density restriction policy for natural area preservation exists, other than the general policies found in the General Plan. Land purchase appears to be the protection technique that the County has used most extensively for ESA protection.

No definitions or criteria for the words 'unique natural areas' and 'unique and representative ecological areas' have been developed. This affects the delineation of the areas and can create confusion during legal or political approval processes. The lack of an inventory of all such natural areas in the County limits the effectiveness of the policy plans.

Conclusions

Montgomery County is a wealthy county with a mature and sophisticated planning structure. The rapid development in the postwar period combined with an environmental awareness in the populace has created a milieu in which environmental planning has developed and matured. Concern for natural area protection is woven throughout the County General Plan.

The scientific bases for environmental management, accurate resource data, advanced analytical techniques and competent staff are present in the United States. Montgomery County is fortunate in this regard because of the nearby presence of many federal government agencies and the associated expert staff resources.

The taking issue limits the ability of municipal governments to develop a balanced plan that has a range of development from high density through to completely natural. The reasons for the success of Montgomery County in protecting its natural communities have been summarized by R. Tustian, the Planning Director:

> One of the reasons that I believe we have been as successful as we have in avoiding reversals by the courts, is that we have been prudent, and have tried to evolve our management strategies and techniques in an organic way from a base of pre-existing and accepted practices. Within this context, we have threaded our concern for environmental protection through all our planning vehicles, so as to produce a hierarchy of interrelated points where environmental sensitivity can be evaluated, rather than putting boundaries around a limited number of ESA's (pers. comm.).

Such an approach requires constant data collection, monitoring and assessment by a multi-disciplinary staff. The court cases in the last decade that established the authority of municipalities to control density, the need of developers to show that land-use change is not ecologically damaging, and the desirability of having regard for the protection of natural environmental resources should give municipal planning authorities more direct tools to protect natural areas in the US in the future.

Summary

The planning and management of natural ecosystems by local levels of government is an emerging policy development in Europe, Asia and North America. Each of the municipalities studied has developed a unique set of institutional arrangements for the local legal and political environment that is present. Postwar economic development has caused widespread land-use change. A cadre of professionally-trained land-use planners has become part of municipal administration. The need to conserve ecological diversity and the productive capability of ecosystems has become more apparent as the amount of natural area has declined. As a result, a widespread recognition of the important role of local municipalities has developed.

The regional-level municipal governments are in the forefront of this policy development. They have been much more successful in developing and in implementing natural heritage conservation policies than have local municipalities – cities, towns and townships. This suggests that a regional approach has some optimum balance of public accountability and resource scale. The county is sufficiently close to local opinion for conservation policies to be implemented with a general community agreement. Conversely, it is far enough away from individuals for difficult land-use allocations to be made. The general community need for ecological management can supersede the disbenefit that results to certain individuals. Most Environmentally Sensitive Areas require regional-level consideration for inventory, delineation and management. The areas are often too large for adequate consideration by one municipality. They cross municipal boundaries, are influenced by regional watersheds and airsheds and are best understood as a component of a regional ecosystem.

Japan is advanced in having a nation-wide survey of the natural environment. This 'national green census' enables decision makers to place individual pieces of property, ecological communities and species into an objective framework for quantitative determination. Britain is not far behind with its many atlas surveys of individual species. Canada and the US have only a few widespread inventories.

In three countries, Britain, Japan and Canada, the municipal governments have the clear legal authority to regulate the degree of development allowed on private land. The protection of Environmentally Sensitive Areas has also been recognized as a valid cause for the use of this development restriction power. However, the negative political response of such a limitation can be important enough to limit its use and effectiveness. The private landowners in Japan and Britain are more willing to accept the limitation for a common good than are those in Canada. In the United States the taking issue has limited the capability of local governments to apply development restrictions for ecological purposes. Court decisions in the last decade have started to change this situation into one similar to those in the other countries studied.

The institutional arrangements developed in Canada are possibly the most sophisticated of those studied. Specifically, the criteria and inventory methods used for delineation are novel. In addition, the use of a technical advisory committee composed of professional experts ensures that the political process gets competent advice based on defensible facts.

It is significant that the conservation of local ecosystems has been recognized so widely at the local level in a number of countries. The evolution of these programmes has taken place simultaneously but relatively independently. The framers of the World Conservation Strategy (International Union for Conservation of Nature and Natural Resources, 1980) can take heart at the advanced degree of environmental management that has recently started to develop in municipal governments in these developed countries.

133

CHAPTER 7

The future

A summary

One of the most striking observations made during the research for this book was that a policy initiative with regard to ESA planning was taking place *independently* in all four countries studied. There appears to be a widespread organic development of the concept at the municipal level. The evidence suggests that the theoretical constructs of applied ecology are being applied by a cadre of professional planners at the local governmental level with the support of a large proportion of the local populace. In Britain and Japan the national governments are providing encouragement in the form of advice, some monetary compensation and importantly large data bases, such as flora and fauna atlases, that make possible the objective determination of constructs such as variety, distribution and size. In Canada and the United States the municipalities are usually going it alone. A few states, such as Maine and Illinois, have state-wide inventory programmes producing information that can be used by municipalities (Hoose 1981) but only one Canadian province, Ontario, has any such programme.

Are the programmes successful in protecting significant natural areas? The answer is certainly a qualified yes. In the last two decades very considerable progress has been made as a sophisticated policy structure for the protection of important natural areas has been developed and implemented. But many significant sites are still being lost. Let us look at various components of the programmes (Table 7.1).

Great Britain definitely has the most advanced inventory and policy implementation structure. The biological data bases are functioning. The SSSI inventory and delineation programme is second to none. The national system of conservation planning which places at least one resource planner in every county has no equal elsewhere. But this small country appears to be losing local natural areas faster than any of the others studied. Even with the advanced resource management system in place the development pressures of all types, and especially from the agricultural and forestry sectors,

Table 7.1 Comparison of policy initiatives

Comparison criteria	Countries	Relative amount		
		poor	satisfactory	excellent
1. Amount of national environmental data available	Britain			X
	Japan		X	
	Canada	X		
	United States		X	
2. Amount of applied ecology research underway	Britain			X
	Japan		X	
	Canada	X		
	United States			X
3. Degree of inventory of local ESAs	Britain			X
	Japan		X	
	Canada			X
	United States	X		
4. National government encouragement	Britain			X
	Japan			X
	Canada	X		
	United States	X		
5. Legal ability of municipalities to limit development	Britain		X	
	Japan			X
	Canada		X	
	United States	X		
6. Political acceptability of ESA–based restrictions	Britain		X	
	Japan			X
	Canada		X	
	United States	X		
7. Degree of policy development by municipalities	Britain			X
	Japan		X	
	Canada		X	
	United States	X		
8. Degree of acceptance of ESAs by local planners	Britain			X
	Japan		X	
	Canada		X	
	United States		X	
9. Degree of citizen involvement in ESA planning	Britain			X
	Japan		X	
	Canada		X	
	United States		X	
10. Amount of loss of local natural areas in last two decades	Britain		X	
	Japan		X	
	Canada			X
	United States		X	

are partly overwhelming the conservation efforts. But one gets the feeling that the British are starting to stem the tide of destruction.

Japan has a very sophisticated national data base for vegetation that has a 1 km grid cell size. The mountainous terrain combined with a long tradition of respect for natural vegetation has resulted in a large amount of the country remaining in a natural or semi-natural state. Western-influenced cultural changes in the last few decades may be resulting in a decreased emphasis on the protection of natural environment by the average citizen. Japan does not now have a country-wide policy thrust of protecting natural areas by local municipalities but many are doing it on their own. But their various park systems protect a larger portion of the country than in any of the areas studied. This national government influence is partially dictated by the relatively small size of the country. One must always keep the fact in mind that Japan and Britain are smaller than the majority of provinces in Canada and states in the US.

Canada has one of the better records of protecting local natural areas, largely due to the large size of the country and small population. Since 1970 a policy thrust for the protection of local ESAs has spread throughout the settled portions of the Province of Ontario and is now being considered in the rapidly developing urban areas of Alberta (City of Calgary 1979) and British Columbia (Greater Vancouver Regional District 1980). This development has widespread public acceptance but considerable resistance from the development industry is being felt in some areas. Canada has a relatively poor national data base for environmental planning. Very recently the compilation of flora and fauna atlases has started (Laughlin, Kibbe and Eagles 1982) but it will take years and possibly decades before even the settled portions of the country will be completed.

The United States is a large and diverse country. Generally, it can be stated that many municipal governments are now having regard for significant local natural areas in their land-use planning. No national policy initiative is taking place but some state governments are moving in this direction. The taking issue, which is a uniquely American situation, hangs over all of the efforts to protect natural areas on private land by the use of planning or zoning controls. Over the last decade the courts have started to recognize the protection of natural landscapes as a valid public policy but the situation is legally quite different from that found in the other countries. Politically, the situation in the US is similar to that in Canada and Britain. That is, private landowners often take exception to the act of a government which limits their 'development' potentials. The US has a moderately good national data base that can be used for environmental planning. For example, several national wetland inventories have been completed. In addition, many state-wide flora and fauna inventories are completed and others are underway.

It is probable that the ESA policy initiative will broaden and deepen in the decades to come. Those factors which suggest this trend include: a rapidly maturing cadre of professional environment planners is spreading through first world governments; the general public is now aware of the Spaceship Earth concept and is aware of the need to preserve ecological diversity; municipal governments are now cognizant of the role they can play in environmental planning and management; as energy costs limit travel, local environments suitable for outdoor recreation become more desirable; and, the field of applied ecology is continuing its rapid development of the theoretical basis on which prescriptive rules for planning and management can be based. Elements which may limit the effectiveness of this initiative include: a shrinking of government activity due to fiscal restraint; an increase in urban density due to energy costs that will heavily impact the remaining natural areas; an enlarging agricultural industry which will result in the loss of natural ecosystems and their replacement by crops; and, legal restrictions on the ability of local governments to preserve ecosystems through development control.

It would be useful to have some mechanism developed that can provide a continual communication between municipal authorities on this subject. This book will hopefully fulfil this purpose at this time but it may not fulfil all of the communication needs in the longer term. The cross-fertilization of ideas can have nothing but a positive benefit to all concerned with the long-term protection of natural areas.

Research questions

Several major research questions emerge from the analyses that went into this book. Two levels of problem-solving are obvious, the theoretical and the applied. It might be reasonable to discuss the research implications under the four basic components described in Chapter 3: ecology, technology, attitudes and institutional arrangements.

Ecologists must continue their work in the fields of island biogeography and impact prediction. The theory of island biogeography is a very useful design tool. The next stage of research should concentrate on refining the predictive models so that we can accurately estimate the size of area needed for the long-term sustainment of individual species and of complete ecosystems. This science is advancing rapidly and, we hope, will continue to do so.

Technology will continue to develop chemicals, machines and processes that will impact on natural ecosystems, often negatively. The local land-use planner is in the front line of environmental policy development and implementation. This person needs relatively simple tools that are cost effective and capable of use in a small office. The advent of the microcomputer at a low cost makes it possible for most planning offices to have access to a sophisticated analytical tool. Here lies a tremendous potential. If senior levels of government would take it upon themselves to develop environmental data bases that could be tapped by a local planner in his own office then his ability to analyse complicated environmental problems would be increased by several orders of magnitude. For example, if he were presented with a land-use proposal that had environmental implications it would be ideal if he could have information on the soils, slopes, vegetation, wildlife and other features made available almost instantaneously from a centralized data bank or a data network. General predictive models could be made available to answer questions such as:

1. How much area of suitable habitat does species X require for survival?
2. Will species Y be removed if 50 per cent of a certain habitat is removed?
3. Is there normally a relationship between soil type Z and vegetation community W?

The potential for expanding the capability of a planner with such a system is immense.

In the four countries studied for this book and in most first world countries there appears to be an emerging consensus that environmental protection is both necessary and desirable. The general public is now familiar with the Spaceship Earth analogy and therefore expects that individuals and institutions act in an environmentally suitable fashion. In the United States public surveys show conclusively that a healthy economy and a healthy environment are both high priority public policy goals (Continental Group 1982). There appears to be a shift away from the dominionistic-utilitarian view of nature to the ecologistic view. This, of course, should assist the environmental managers in their work.

Work must go forward in the policy field of senior governments. In some ways they have some catching up to do, compared to many municipalities. In Japan, Canada and the United States the senior governments need to recognize explicitly the initiatives of the municipalities in ESA planning and management. Small changes in legislation, plan approval processes and grant programmes could help considerably to create a positive atmosphere for the municipal actions. It is essential that the senior levels of governments take action towards the development of environmental data bases.

The progress made so far in ESA planning and management suggests that municipalities with the assistance of senior governments and the encouragement of citizens have a positive contribution to make in environmental management generally and natural area protection specifically. In the future we will probably see a broadening of the application of this concept to more areas and a deepening of our understanding of the effects that local policy processes can have on the protection of ecological diversity.

APPENDIX 1

An SSSI Map and Inventory from the County of Gwent, Wales

An example of an SSSI mapping and description from the Nature Conservancy Council inventory for the County of Gwent. This Government agency produces documents, for each county, that illustrate and describe the National Nature Reserves (NNR) declared under section 19 of the National Parks and Access to the Countryside Act 1949, the Local Nature Reserves (LNR) declared under section 21 of the Act and Sites of Special Scientific Interest (SSSI) under section 23 of the Act. The woods are located on steep slopes along the Wye Valley.

Source: Nature Conservancy Council undated (b)

GWENT   BLACKCLIFF-WYNDCLIFF SSSI

Monmouth District

Date of Notification: 1971

National Grid Reference: ST 531979
  O.S. 1:50,000 Sheet No: 162
    1:25,000 Sheet No: ST 59

Site area: 119.3 hectares (294.8 acres)

Description:
Partially vegetated Carboniferous Limestone cliffs and native woodlands.
The ancient semi-natural high forest and old coppice-with standards contain
important examples of calcareous woodland types with many rare or local
plants in the ground flora. The relict beech (*Fagus sylvatica*) coppice above
Blackcliff is a particularly fine example of this woodland type and the
small-leaved lime (*Tilia cordata*) stands in Wyndcliff are some of the best
examples in the Wye Valley. The many subordinate tree and shrub species
include a number of hybrids of *Sorbus* including *Sorbus aria* × *Sorbus
aucuparia*.

Remarks:
Within the Wye Valley Area of Outstanding Natural Beauty.
Subject to a Forest Nature Reserve Agreement with the Forestry
Commission.
Previously part of the larger Blackcliff-Wyndcliff – Pierce Woods SSSI.

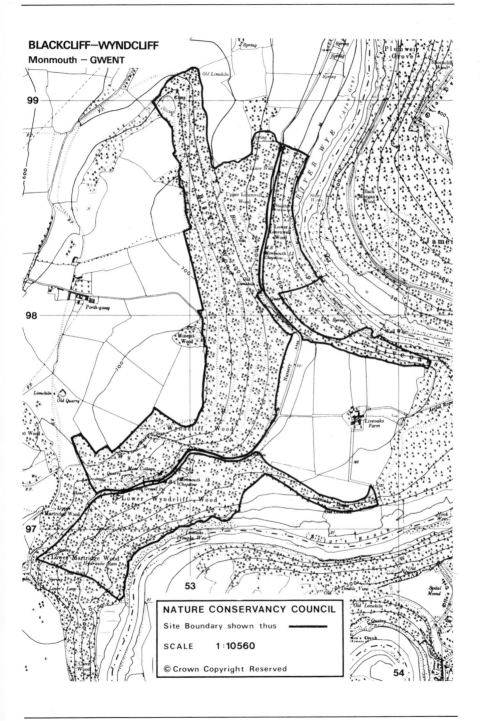

BLACKCLIFF—WYNDCLIFF
Monmouth — GWENT

NATURE CONSERVANCY COUNCIL

Site Boundary shown thus ————

SCALE 1:10560

© Crown Copyright Reserved

An ESA Map and Inventory from Halton County, Ontario

This appendix presents an example of an ESA inventory carried out by the Ecological and Environmental Advisory Committee for the Region of Halton. This local, unpaid advisory committee undertook the inventory and writing of the document. Funding was obtained from the Provincial Ministry of the Environment for student assistance in the summer. The document was presented to the Regional Government in an effort to encourage the protection of the ESAs through municipal planning controls. Sassafras Woods is located in a valley just below the cliff brow of the Niagara Escarpment. Sassafras (*Sassafras albidum*) is an uncommon southern tree that is at the northern edge of its range in Halton.
Source: Region of Halton 1978a

HALTON REGION   E.E.A.C.
ENVIRONMENTALLY SENSITIVE AREA STUDY

SASSAFRAS WOODS   E.S.A. N⁰ 4

Photo Courtesy of Royal Botanical Gardens

General Description

Sassafras Woods supports a secondary growth hardwood
forest overstoried with mature White Pine on a gentle
south-facing slope. This is One of the few remaining
sizeable woodlots typical of the woodland that once
covered most of the Region south of the Escarpment
(W. Crins, Pers. comm. 1976). Five small valley
systems extend into the area along a north-south axis
producing a profile of plateaus alternating with
shallow depressions. Soils are deep red clay. The
forests of the plateau are quite immature but become more
mature in the depressions. Sugar Maple is dominant,
with Shagbark Hickory, Witch Hazel, American Hornbeam,
and Red Oak well represented. This relatively large
woodlot is transected by three hydro lines.

HALTON REGION   **E.E.A.C.**
ENVIRONMENTALLY SENSITIVE AREA STUDY

E.S.A. № **4**

Criteria Fulfilled

Criterion Four:

The long growing season and the immaturity of sections
of Sassafras Woods provide suitable conditions for
Carolinian species such as Sassafras (Sassafras
albidum), Eastern Flowering Dogwood (Cornus florida),
and Common Hoptree (Ptelea trifoliata). This woods
contains the largest number and best quality of
Sassafras and Flowering Dogwood in Halton Region.
These Carolinian species are near the northern limit
of their range in Ontario. Thus their presence
indicates a very unusual habit at for Halton Region. (P.
Maycock, Pers. comm. 1976).

Criterion Six:

The most significant plant species found is Common
Hoptree (Ptelea trifoliata). Not only is this tree
considered nationally rare and provincially rare,
but it may be the only known spontaneous specimen in
Halton Region (P.F. Rice, Pers. comm.)

A number of other nationally and provincially rare
plants are found:

>   American Columbo (Swertia caroliniensis)
>   Eastern Flowering Dogwood (Cornus florida)
>   Large-bracted Tick Trefoil (Desmodium cuspidatum)
>   Honey Locust (Gleditsia triacanthos)
>   Red Hickory (Carya ovalis)

Sassafras albidum, a nationally significant species,
is represented by a healthy colony of about 25 trees
reaching heights of 35 feet. Also found in the area
is Yellow Ladies' Slipper (Cypripedium calceolus) and
Three-leaved False Solomon's Seal (Smilacina trifolia),
both regionally rare.

Uncommon birds include Whip Poor-will (Caprimulgus
vociferus), Golden-crowned Kinglet (Regulus satrapa),
and Ruby-crowned Kinglet (Regulus calendula). (M.
Ilyniak, Pers. comm. 1977).

E.S.A. № **4**

HALTON REGION

E.E.A.C.

ENVIRONMENTALLY SENSITIVE AREA STUDY

E.S.A. No **4**

General Comments

At present the major impact on the area is noise.
Traffic from Highway #403 and North Service Road, as
well as trail bikes in the eastern section of the
woodlot, are major contributors. The trail bikes
have also created local soil disturbances and trampled
vegetation, especially on the east side of the western
valley. This unnecessary destruction of habitat is
a continuing problem and may seriously deface the
woodlot if it is not curtailed.

Another impact may come from residential development
which currently is concentrated along the western
valley.

Sassafras Woods may not be well protected because of
its private ownership, proximity to a major traffic
artery, and its "Complementary Use" designation within
the Parkway Belt West Plan. The Ontario Land Inventory
has classified the most easterly valley as hazard land.

One of the last remaining sizeable woodlots below the
Escarpment, this part of the Region should be protected
from the adverse affects of development and from
abuse by trail bikes. The eastern-most valley with
its fairly mature sugar maple forest extending to
connect Sassafras Woods to the Waterdown Escarpment
Woods provides a good linkage between the two areas.
The only separation between them is a large hydro
corridor, which should be revegetated to reduce the
obstacle for mammals and birds.

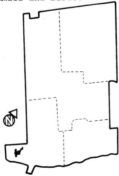

E.S.A. No **4**

HALTON REGION
E.E.A.C.
ENVIRONMENTALLY SENSITIVE AREA STUDY

SASSAFRAS WOODS
E.S.A. Nº 4

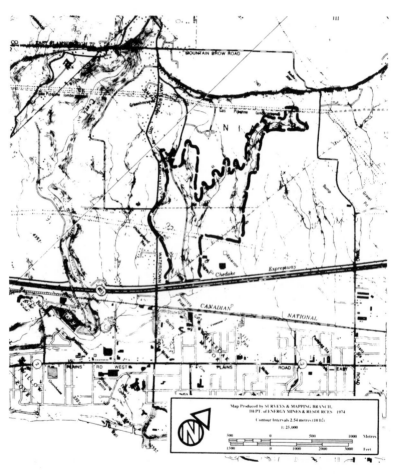

E.S.A. Nº 4

References

Abrassart, A. E. and D. D. McFarlane (1974) 'The economics of environmental preservation: Comment', *The American Economic Review* **64** (6): 1025–9.

Adirondack Park Agency (1979b) *Rules and Regulations*, Ray Brook, New York. New York, 65 pp.

Adirondack Park Agency (1979b) *Rules and Regulations* Ray Brook, New York. 150 pp.

Adirondack Park Agency (1980) *APA Act*, Ray Brook, New York, 65 pp.

Alden, H. R. (1982) 'Citizen involvement in gravel pit reclamation: A case study', in W. D. Svedarsky and R. D. Crawford, *Wildlife Values of Gravel Pits*, pp. 95–101, Miscellaneous Publication 17–1982, Agricultural Experiment Station, University of Minnesota, St Paul, Minnesota. 249 pp.

Andreski, S. (1972) *Social Sciences as Sorcery*, St Martin's Press, New York. 238 pp.

Anonymous (1977a) 'Bird breeding aims at higher survival in wild', *Endangered Species Technical Bulletin* **2** (11): 6–8.

Anonymous (1977b) 'A VIP escort for migrating whoopers', *Endangered Species Technical Bulletin* **2** (12): 4.

Anonymous (1978a) '9 areas designated whooping crane critical habitat', *Endangered Species Technical Bulletin* **3** (6): 6.

Anonymous (1978b) 'Unique gravel pit features golfing and fishing', *Interface* **1** (1): 1.

Arbib, R. (1976) 'The Blue List for 1977', *American Birds* **30** (6): 1031–9.

Argus, G. W. and D. J. White (1982) *Atlas of the Rare Vascular Plants of Ontario*, Botany Division, National Museum of Natural Sciences, Ottawa, Ontario. 23 pp. plus species sheets for Cyperaceae, Liliaceae and Orchidaceae.

Armour, E. M., L. Lawrence and M. White (1979) *Field Study of Environmentally Sensitive Areas in Halton*, Regional Municipality of Halton Planning Department, Oakville, Ontario. 107 pp.

Batisse, M. (1971) 'Man and biosphere: An international research programme', *Biological Conservation* **4** (1): 1–6.

Baum, P. W. (1976) 'Towards the setting up of a European network of biogenetic reserves', *Naturopa* **25**: 11–13.

Beechey, T. J. and R. J. Davidson (1980) 'Protection of provincially significant wildlife areas', in S. Barrett and J. Riley, *Protection of Natural Areas in Ontario*,

References

pp. 20–49, Working Paper No. 3, Faculty of Environmental Studies, York University, Downsview, Ontario. 185 pp.

Bishop, R. C. (1976) 'Review of *The Economics of Natural Environments* by Krutilla and Fisher', *Land Economics* **52** (4): 567–72.

Bishop, R. C. (1978) 'Endangered species and uncertainty: the economics of a safe minimum standard', *American Journal of Agricultural Economics* **60** (1): 10–18.

Bos, W., L. Brisson and P. Eagles (1977) *A Study of Attitudinal Orientations of Central Canadian Cultures towards Wildlife*, Project No. 702–17 Waterloo Research Institute, University of Waterloo, Waterloo, Ontario. 126 pp.

Bosselman, F. P. (1975) 'Property rights in land: new statutory approaches', *Natural Resources Journal* **15** (4): 681–93.

Brady, R. F., T. Tobias, P. F. J. Eagles, R. Ohrner, J. Micak, B. Veale and R. S. Dorney (1979) 'A typology for the urban ecosystem and its relationship to larger biogeographical landscape units', *Urban Ecology* **4**: 11–28.

Bray, J. A. D. and G. S. Probert (1981) *Gwent Structure Plan – Written Statement of Policies and Proposals*, Gwent County Council, County Hall, Cwmbran, Gwent. 272 pp. plus appendices.

Brobst, B. K. and P. F. J. Eagles (1977) *An Environmentally Sensitive Area Management Study – Irish Creek Forest*, School of Urban and Regional Planning, University of Waterloo, Waterloo, Ontario. 67 pp.

Catchpole, C. K. and C. F. Tydeman (1975) 'Gravel pits as new wetland habitats for the conservation of breeding bird communities', *Biological Conservation* **8**: 47–59.

Catling, C. K., J. E. Cruise, K. L. McIntosh, and S. M. McKay (1975) 'Alvar vegetation in Southern Ontario', *Ontario Field Biologist* **29** (2): 1–25.

Chanasyk, V. (1970) *The Haldimand-Norfolk Appraisal*, Ontario Ministry of Treasury, Economics and Intergovernmental Affairs, Toronto, Ontario. Volumes 1 and 2. 263 pp. plus maps.

Ciriacy-Wantrup, S. V. and R. C. Bishop (1975) ' "Property" as a concept in natural resources policy', *Natural Resources Journal* **15** (4): 713–27.

City of Calgary (1979) *A Policy for Environmentally Sensitive Areas*, Planning and Parks/Recreation Departments, Calgary, Alberta. 17 pp.

Coates, W. E. (1976) 'How to recover a quarry', *Bulletin of the Conservation Council of Ontario* **23** (3): 4–7.

Coleman, L. and P. E. Perrine (1982) 'Homegrown TDR', *Planning* **48** (1): 15–17.

Commoner, B. (1971) *The environmental cost of economic growth*, paper presented at the Resources For the Future Forum on Energy; Economic growth and the environment. Washington DC.

Continental Group (1982) *Toward Responsible Growth: Economic and Environmental Concern in the Balance*. The Continental Group Inc., Stamford, Connecticut. 179 pp.

Correll, M. R., J. H. Lillydahl and L. D. Singell (1978) 'The effects of greenbelts on residential property values: some findings on the political economy of open space', *Land Economics* **54** (2): 207–17.

Crockett, J. U. and O. E. Allen (1977) *Wildflower Gardening*, Time-Life Books, Alexandria, Virginia. 160 pp.

Crowe, R. B., G. A. McKay and W. M. Baker (1977) *The Tourist and Outdoor Recreation Climate of Ontario*, (3 volumes) Atmospheric Environment Service, Environment Canada, Ottawa.

Cummings, R. and V. Norton (1974) 'The economics of environmental preservation: comment', *The American Economic Review* **64** (6): 1021–4.

Dansereau, P. (1977) *Harmony and Disorder in the Canadian Environment*, Canadian Environmental Advisory Council, Ottawa. Occasional Paper No. 1. 145 pp.

Dasmann, R. F., J. P. Milton and P. F. Freeman (1973) *Ecological Principles for Economic Development*, John Wiley, London. 252 pp.

Davis, A. M. and T. F. Gleck (1978) 'Urban ecosystems and island biogeography', *Environmental Conservation* **5** (4): 299–304.

Department of the Environment (1972) *Structure and Local Plans – Your Opportunity*, HMSO, London. 4 pp.

Department of the Environment (1973) *Structure Plans. The Examination in Public.* HMSO, London. 12 pp.

Department of Lands, Forests and Water Resources (1975) *Ecological Reserves in British Columbia*, Province of British Columbia, Victoria. 8 pp.

Desmond, F., and G. Vessey-Fitz (1974) 'In a state of naturalness', *Environmental Conservation* **1** (3): 231–2.

Diamond, J. M. (1975) 'The island dilemma: lessons of modern biogeographic studies for the design of natural reserves', *Biological Conservation* **7**: 129–45.

Diamond, J. M. (1976) 'Island biogeography: strategy and limitations', *Science* **193**: 1027–9.

Diamond, J. M. and R. M. May (1976) 'Island biogeography and the design of natural reserves', in R. M. May, *Theoretical Ecology*, pp. 163–86, Blackwell Scientific Publications, London. 317 pp.

Diekelmann, J. and R. Schuster (1982) *Natural Landscaping*, McGraw-Hill, Toronto, Ontario. 276 pp.

Dietmann, A. J. and A. E. Giraldi (1974) *A Provisional Inventory of the Flora and Fauna of Seneca Creek, Muddy Branch, and Watts Branch Watersheds, Montgomery County, Maryland*, Maryland-National Park and Planning Commission, Montgomery County, Silver Spring, Maryland. 87 pp.

DiResta, A. E. (1982) 'Environmental regulation/constitutional law – "taking" jurisprudence and its application to regulations of sensitive ecological environments', *Florida State University Law Review* **9**: 489–512.

Dorfman, R. and N. S. Dorfman (1972) *Economics of the Environment: Selected Readings*, Norton, New York. 426 pp.

Dorney, R. S. (1975) 'Re-creating the early Ontario landscape in a front yard', *Landscape Architecture* **65**: 420–23.

Dorney, R. S. and M. G. George (1970) *An Ecological Analysis of the Waterloo-South Wellington Region*, Division of Environmental Studies, University of Waterloo, Waterloo, Ontario. 202 pp.

Dorney, R. S. (1977a) 'Environmental assessment: the ecological dimension', *Journal of the American Water Works Association* **69** (4): 182–5.

Dorney, R. S. (1977b) 'The mini-ecosystem', *Journal of Landscape Architecture of Canada* **3** (4): 56–61.

Dorney, R. S. and D. W. Hoffman (1979) 'Development of landscape planning concepts and management strategies for an urbanizing agricultural region', *Landscape Planning* **6**: 151–77.

Dorney, R. S. and S. E. Amster (1980) *Environmental Management of the Urban Ecosystem in Southern Ontario*, Geographical Interuniversity Resource Manage-

References

ment Seminar **10**: 41–65. Department of Geography, Wilfrid Laurier University, Waterloo, Ontario.

Drury, G. H. (1973) *The British Isles*, Heinemann Educational, London. 365 pp.

Duncan, O. D. (1976) 'Social organization and the ecosystem', in P. J. Richardson and J. McEvoy, *Human Ecology – An Environmental Approach*, pp. 26–68, Duxbury Press, North Scituate, Massachusetts. 370 pp.

Eagles, P. F. J. (1976) 'A study of breeding bird populations in Bronte Creek Provincial Park', unpublished M.Sc. thesis, Department of Zoology, University of Guelph, Guelph, Ontario. 105 pp.

Eagles, P. F. J., W. Elrick, D. Foster, S. Muirhead, M. Stewart, J. Van de Hulst and C. Waterston (1976) *South Wellington Environmentally Sensitive Areas Study*, Centre for Resources Development, Publication No. 79. University of Guelph, Guelph, Ontario. 212 pp.

Eagles, P. F. J. and T. N. Tobias (1978) 'A replication of a breeding bird census', *American Birds* **32** (1): 14–17.

Eagles, P. F. J. (1979) 'The institutional arrangements for Environmentally Sensitive Area planning and management in Ontario', unpublished Ph.D. thesis, School of Urban and Regional Planning, University of Waterloo, Waterloo, Ontario. 352 pp.

Eagles, P. F. J. (1980a) 'An approach to describing recreation in the natural environment', *Recreation Research Review* **8** (1): 28–36.

Eagles, J. (1980b) 'Criteria for the designation of Environmentally Sensitive Areas', in S. Barrett and J. Riley, *Protection of Natural Areas in Ontario*, pp. 68–79, Working Paper No. 3, Faculty of Environmental Studies, York University, Downsview, Ontario. 185 pp.

Eagles, P. F. J. (1981) 'Environmentally Sensitive Area planning in Ontario, Canada', *American Planning Association Journal* **47** (3): 313–23.

Eagles, P. F. J., D. Bronson, B. Adam, B. Botman, C. Braithwaite, L. Calvert, H. Dawson, M. deVries, D. Dickie, J. Foss, L. Horrocks, S. Mandel, D. Manoochehri, J. McCauley, D. McIsaac, P. Nichols, C. Reid, B. Roelofson, M. Sjonnesen and K. Zavitz (1981) *The Feasibility of Establishing a National Park in the Bruce Peninsula and Manitoulin Island Area of Ontario*, Department of Recreation, University of Waterloo, Waterloo, Ontario. 147 pp.

Eagles, P. F. J. (1982) 'Gravel pit reclamation in Ontario: the Crieff case study', in W. D. Svedarsky and R. D. Crawford, *Wildlife Values of Gravel Pits*, pp. 141–9, Miscellaneous Publication 17–1982, Agricultural Experiment Station, University of Minnesota, St Paul, Minnesota. 249 pp.

Eagles, P. F. J. and M. Gewurz (1982) *The Natural Resources of the Fletcher Creek Swamp Forest Conservation Area*, Department of Recreation, University of Waterloo, Waterloo, Ontario. 231 pp.

Ecologistics (1979) *Credit River Watershed Environmentally Significant Areas*, Credit Valley Conservation Authority, Meadowvale, Ontario. 207 pp.

Ettinger, W. and C. Yuill (1982) 'Sand and gravel pit reclamation in Louisiana: creation of wetlands habitat and its integration into adjacent undisturbed bayou', in W. D. Svedarsky and R. D. Crawford, *Wildlife Values of Gravel Pits*, pp. 109–14, Miscellaneous Publication 17–1982, Agricultural Experiment Station, University of Minnesota, St Paul, Minnesota. 249 pp.

Ferriday, A. (1961) *A Regional Geography of the British Isles*, Macmillan, London. 361 pp.

Fisher, A. C., J. V. Krutilla and C. J. Cicchetti (1972) 'The economics of environmental preservation: a theoretical and empirical analysis', *The American Economic Review*, **62** (4): 605–19.

Fisher, A. C., J. V. Krutilla and C. J. Cicchetti (1974) 'The economics of environmental preservation: further discussion', *The American Economic Review*, **64** (6): 1030–39.

Fossel, C. (1973) *The Nature Wardens of Austria*, Bulletin of the European Information Centre for Nature Conservation, Council of Europe 14: 25.

Francis, G. R. and P. F. J. Eagles (eds) (1975) *A Study of the Environmentally Sensitive Areas for the Environmental Policy Plan of the Regional Municipality of Waterloo*, Department of Man-Environment Studies, University of Waterloo, Waterloo, Ontario. 99 pp.

Francis, G. R. (1977) 'Pieces of green – a regional policy to protect remnant natural areas', *Ontario Naturalist* **17** (4): 12–19.

Francis, G. R. (1978) 'Some perspectives on conserving a system of remnant natural areas in southern Ontario', in S. Hilts, *Natural Areas: Identification, Dedication and Management*, pp. 43–75, GIRMS Special Publication No. 1, Department of Geography, Wilfrid Laurier University, Waterloo, Ontario. 90 pp.

Franklin, J. F., F. C. Hall, C. T. Dyrness and C. Maser (1972) *Federal Research Natural Areas in Oregon and Washington – A Guidebook for Scientists and Educators*, Pacific Northwest Forest and Range Experimental Station, Forest Service, US Department of Agriculture, Portland, Oregon. 488 pp.

Galli, A. E., C. F. Leck and R. T. T. Forman (1976) 'Avian distribution patterns in forest islands of different sizes in central New Jersey', *Auk* **93**: 356–64.

Glue, D. E. (1970) 'Changes in the bird community of a Hampshire gravel pit 1963–68, *Bird Study* **17**: 15–27.

Goeden, G. B. (1979) 'Biogeographic theory as a management tool', *Environmental Conservation* **6** (1): 27–32.

Goode, D. (undated) *Recent Losses of Wildlife Habitats in Britain*, Nature Conservancy Council, London, 6 pp.

Goode, D. (1981) 'The threat to wildlife habitats', *New Scientist* **22**: 219–23.

Gorrie, A. M. (1969) *A Geography of Japan*, Nelson, Melbourne. 198 pp.

Grampian Regional Council (1980) *Sites of Interest to Natural Science*, Study of Environmentally Sensitive Areas, Department of Physical Planning, Aberdeen. 24 pp.

Greater Vancouver Regional District (1980) *Plan for the Lower Mainland of British Columbia*, Central Fraser Valley, Dewdney – Alouette, Greater Vancouver and Fraser-Cheam Regional Districts, Vancouver, British Columbia. 106 pp.

Hardin, G. (1968) 'The tragedy of the commons', *Science*, **162**: 1243–8.

Harrington, F. (1977) *A Guide to the Mammals of Iran*, Department of the Environment, Tehran. 88 pp.

Harrison, J. and J. Harrison (1972) 'Gravel-pit management for wildfowl and other birds', in E. Dennis, *Everyman's Nature Reserve – Ideas for Action*, pp. 217–33, David and Charles, Newton Abbot, 256 pp.

Harrison, P. and J. Harrison (1976) 'The management of an English gravel pit waterfowl reserve', *Naturopa* **24**: 15–17.

Hill, G. (1982) 'California's coastal commission: ten years of triumphs, *Planning* **48** (1): 10–14.

References

Hills, A. G., D . V. Douglas, and S. Locate (1973) *Developing a Better Environment: A Study of Methodology in the Development of Regional Plans*, The Ontario Economic Council, Toronto, Ontario. 182 pp.

Hoose, P. M. (1981) *Building An Ark*, Island Press, Covelo, California. 221 pp.

HUDAC (Housing and Urban Development Association of Canada) (1978a) *Environmental Assessment Requirements and New Housing Projects*, 27 pp. (mimeo)

HUDAC (Housing and Urban Development Association of Canada) (1978b) *Environmental Assessment Requirements and New Housing Projects in Waterloo Region*, submission to Council of the Corporation of the Regional Municipality of Waterloo and to the Palmer Commission on Local Government Review. 40 pp.

Hull, H. S. (ed) (1976) 'Gardening with wild flowers', *Plants and Gardens* **18** (1): 1–97.

International Bee Research Association (1980) *Atlas of the Bumblebees of the British Isles*, Biological Records Centre, Huntingdon. 32 pp.

International Union for the Conservation of Nature (1971) *United Nations List of National Parks and Equivalent Reserves*, IUCN International Commission on National Parks, Hayez, Brussels. 601 pp.

International Union for Conservation of Nature and Natural Resources (1980) *World Conservation Strategy*, 1196 Gland, Switzerland.

Jakab, S., L. P. Densmore and S. R. Warren (1980) *Field Study of Environmentally Sensitive Areas in Halton*, Regional Municipality of Halton Planning Department, Oakville, Ontario. 71 pp.

Japan Environment Agency (1976a) *Quality of the Environment in Japan*, International Affairs Division, Tokyo. 240 pp.

Japan Environment Agency (1976b) *National State of Nature Survey Report*, Tokyo. 5 pp.

Japan Environment Agency (1977) *Outline of Nature Conservation Policy in Japan*, 3–1–1 Kasumigaseki, Chiyoda-Ku, Tokyo. 64 pp.

Japan Environment Agency (1981) *Environmental Laws and Regulations in Japan* (IV) *Nature*. Environmental Agency, Tokyo. 102 pp.

Japan National Tourist Organization (1981) *Tourism in Japan*, Department of Tourism, Ministry of Transport, Tokyo. 79 pp.

Japan National Tourist Organization (1982) *Inland Sea National Park*, Department of Tourism, Ministry of Transport, Tokyo. 6 pp.

Kellert, S. R. (1979) *Public Attitudes Toward Critical Wildlife and Natural Habitat Issues*, Phase 1, Fish and Wildlife Service, US Department of the Interior, Washington DC. 137 pp.

Kellert, S. R. (1980a) *Activities of the American Public Relating to Animals*, Phase II, Fish and Wildlife Service, US, Department of the Interior, Washington DC. 177 pp.

Kellert, S. R. (1980b) *Knowledge, Affection and Basic Attitudes Toward Animals in American Society*, Phase III, Fish and Wildlife Service, US Department of the Interior, Washington DC. 162 pp.

Kellert, S. R. (1981) *Trends in Animal Use and Perception in Twentieth-Century America*, Phase IV, Fish and Wildlife Service, US Department of the Interior, Washington DC. 166 pp.

Kelso, M. M. (1976) 'Review of *The Economics of Natural Environments* by Krutilla and Fisher', *Land Economics*, **52** (4): 572–7.

References

Kershow, W. W. (1975) *Land Acquisition*, National Recreation and Park Association, Special Publication 15002, Arlington, Virginia. 26 pp.

Knapp, K. W. (1950) *Social Costs of Private Enterprise*, Harvard University Press, Cambridge, Massachusetts. 287 pp.

Kramer, J. (1973) *Natural Gardens – Gardening with Native Plants*. Charles Scribner's Sons, New York. 150 pp.

Krutilla, J. V. and A. C. Fisher (1975) *The Economics of Natural Environments: Studies in the Valuation of Commodity and Amenity Resources*, Johns Hopkins University, Baltimore. 292 pp.

Kusler, J. A. (1980) *Regulating Sensitive Lands*, Ballinger, Cambridge, Massachusetts. 248 pp.

Laughlin, S., D. P. Kibbe and P. F. J. Eagles (1982) 'Atlasing the distribution of the breeding birds of North America', *American Birds* 36 (1): 6–19.

Lindsey, A. A., D. V. Schmelz and S. A. Nichols (1969) *Natural Areas in Indiana and Their Preservation*, Department of Biological Sciences, Purdue, Lafayette, Indiana. 586 pp.

Lomax, J. L. (1982) 'Wildlife use of mineral, extraction industry sites in the coastal plains of New Jersey, in W. D. Svedarsky and R. D. Crawford, *Wildlife Values of Gravel Pits*, pp. 115–21, Miscellaneous Publication 17–1982, Agricultural Experiment Station, University of Minnesota, St Paul, Minnesota, 249 pp.

Mabey, R. (1980) *The Common Ground*, Hutchinson, London. 280 pp.

MacArthur, R. H. and E. O. Wilson (1967) *The Theory of Island Biogeography*, Princeton University Press, Princeton. 203 pp.

MacClintock, L., R. F. Whitcomb and B. L. Whitcomb (1977) 'Evidence for the value of corridors and minimization of isolation in preservation of biotic diversity', *American Birds* 31 (1): 6–12.

MacNaughton, I. F. (1971) 'An economic and physical examination of urban open space with specific reference to natural floodplain parks', unpublished MA thesis, School of Urban and Regional Planning, University of Waterloo, Waterloo. 144 pp.

Maryland-National Capital Park and Planning Commission (1976) *Preliminary Draft Watershed Concept Plan for Conservation and Management in the Seneca Creek and Muddy Branch Basins*, Montgomery County Regional Office, Silver Spring, Maryland. 89 pp.

McLellan, A. G. (1973) 'Derelict land in Ontario – environmental crime or economic shortsightedness', *Bulletin of the Conservation Council of Ontario* 20 (4): 9–14.

McLellan, A. G., S. E. Yundt and M. L. Dorfman (1979) *Abandoned Pits and Quarries in Ontario*, Ontario Geological Survey, Miscellaneous Paper 79 Toronto, Ontario. 36 pp.

McNelly, T. (1972) *Politics and Government in Japan*, (2nd ed.) Houghton Mifflin, Boston. 276 pp.

Metropolitan Washington Council of Governments (1968) *Natural Features of the Washington Metropolitan Area, Washington DC, United States*. 49 pp.

Miller, G. T. (1975) *Living in the Environment: Concepts, Problems and Alternatives*. Wadsworth Publishing Co., Inc., Belmont, California. 603 pp.

Milne, B. S. (1974) 'Ecological succession and bird-life at a newly excavated gravel pit', *Bird Study* 21: 263–77.

Milne, B. (1975) 'Gravel pit studies', *British Trust for Ornithology News* 72: 1–2.

References

Ministry of Natural Resources (1972) *Bronte Creek Provincial Park Master Plan*, Division of Parks, Queens Park, Toronto, Ontario. 40 pp.

Ministry of Natural Resources (1974) *Statistics*, Queen's Park, Toronto, Ontario. 116 pp.

Ministry of Natural Resources (1981) *Provincial Nature Reserves in Ontario*, Parks and Recreation Branch, Queen's Park, Toronto, Ontario. 21 pp.

Mishan, E. (1967) *The Costs of Economic Growth*, Praeger, New York. 190 pp.

Montgomery County Planning Board (1969) *Updated General Plan for Montgomery County*, Maryland-National Capital Park and Planning Commission, Silver Spring, Maryland. 31 pp.

Montgomery County Planning Board (1978) *Park, Recreation and Open Space Master Plan*, Maryland-National Capital Park and Planning Commission, Silver Spring, Maryland. 146 pp.

Montgomery County Planning Board (1979) *Long Range Forecast: People, Jobs and Housing*, Silver Spring, Maryland. 50 pp.

Moore, N. W. and M. D. Hooper (1975) 'On the number of bird species in British woods', *Biological Conservation* **8**: 239–50.

Mukherjee, A. K. (1966) *The Japanese Political System*, The World Press Private Ltd, Calcutta. 165 pp.

Mulamootil, G. and R. Farvolden (1975) 'Planning for the rehabilitation of gravel pits', *Water Resources Bulletin* **11** (3): 599–604.

National Parks Association of Japan (undated) *Beautiful Nature of Japan*, Tokyo, Japan. 18 pp.

Nature Conservancy (1975) *The Preservation of Natural Diversity: A Survey and Recommendations*, The Nature Conservancy, Arlington, Virginia. 309 pp.

Nature Conservancy Council (undated (a)) *A Review of the County of Gwent*, Regional Office South Wales, Cardiff. 18 pp.

Nature Conservancy Council (undated (b)) *Statutory Sites under the National Parks and Access to the Countryside Act, 1949 – Gwent*, Regional Office South Wales, Cardiff. 110 pp. (mimeo)

Nelson, J. G. (1978) 'Canadian National Parks and related reserves: development, research needs and management', in J. G. Nelson, R. D. Needham, D. L. Mann (eds), *International Experience with National Parks and Related Reserves*, pp. 43–88, Department of Geography, Publication Series No. 12, University of Waterloo, Waterloo, Ontario. 624 pp.

New York State (1976) *Guide to Outdoor Recreation in New York State*, New York State Parks and Recreation, Empire State Plaza, Albany. 2 pp.

Niagara Escarpment Commission (1979) *The Proposed Plan for the Niagara Escarpment*, Georgetown, Ontario. 84 pp. plus maps.

Numata, M. (1982) 'The development of the Chiba Bayshore cities and related ecological problems', in M. Numata (ed.), *Chiba Bay – Coast Cities Project*, pp. 1–17, Faculty of Science, Chiba University, Chiba, Japan. 184 pp.

Odum, E. P. (1971) *Fundamentals of Ecology* (2nd ed.) W. B. Saunders Toronto, Ontario. 574 pp.

Oldenburg, R. C., R. A. Montgomery, T. M. Harder and G. V. Burger (1982) 'Gravel pits as fish and wildlife habitat at the Max McGraw Wildlife Foundation', in W. D. Svedarsky and R. D. Crawford, *Wildlife Values of Gravel Pits*, pp. 215–20, Miscellaneous Publication 17–1982, Agricultural Experiment Station, University of Minnesota, St Paul, Minnesota. 249 pp.

Ottawa Field Naturalists' Club (1970) *Preliminary Recommendations Regarding Zoning for Natural Areas and Wildlife Sanctuaries in the Regional Municipality of Ottawa – Carleton*, brief presented to the Ottawa–Carleton Regional Government, Ottawa.

Paget, G. (1976) *Towards a Theory for Environmental Planning*, Student Discussion Paper Number 2, Faculty of Environmental Studies, York University, Downsview, Ontario. 84 pp.

Parks Canada (1979) *Parks Canada Policy*, Department of the Environment, Ottawa, Ontario. 69 pp.

Parks Canada (1981) *The Protection of Canada's Natural Heritage – Canada's National Parks System*, National Parks Systems Division, Environment Canada, Ottawa, Ontario. 12 pp.

Passmore, J. A. (1974) *Man's Responsibility for Nature: Ecological Problems and Western Traditions*. Duckworth, London. 213 pp.

Paton, D. G. and M. J. Sharp (1979) *A Biological Inventory of Halton Region Conservation Authority Properties*, Halton Region Conservation Authority. Milton. Ontario. 147 pp.

Perring, F. H. and S. M. Walters (1962) *Atlas of the British Flora*, Botanical Society of the British Isles, Nelson, London. 432 pp.

Pickett, S. T. A. and J. N. Thompson (1978) 'Patch dynamics and the design of nature reserves', *Biological Conservation* 13: 27–37.

Pielou, E. C. (1975) *Ecological Diversity*, John Wiley and Sons, New York. 165 pp.

Poore, D. (1975) 'Conservation and development', *Environmental Conservation* 2 (4): 243–6.

Poore, D. and P. Gryn-Ambroes (1980) *Nature Conservation in Northern and Western Europe*, United Nations Environment Programme, International Union for Conservation of Nature and Natural Resources, World Wildlife Fund, Gland, Switzerland. 408 pp.

Poore, M. E. D. (1981) *Planning Reserves in Densely-Populated Areas: Examples from Europe and the Mediterranean Region*, UNESCO/MAB Paper 3/8, Paris. 18 pp.

Pratt, P. D. (1979) *A Preliminary Life Science Inventory of the Ojibway Prairie Complex and Surrounding Area*, City of Windsor and Ontario Ministry of Natural Resources. 163 pp.

Probert, G. (1978) *Gwent Structure Plan – Report of Survey*, Gwent County Council, County Hall, Cwmbran, Gwent, 274 pp. plus appendices.

Ralph, B. and P. F. J. Eagles (1977) *An Environmentally Sensitive Area Management Study – Galt Ridge, Beake Pond*, School of Urban and Regional Planning, University of Waterloo, Waterloo, Ontario. 110 pp.

Ratcliffe, D. (1977) *A Nature Conservation Review*, Cambridge University Press, Cambridge.

Region of Halton (1978) *Environmentally Sensitive Areas Study*, Planning Department, Oakville, Ontario. 261 pp.

Region of Halton (1980) *The Regional Plan*, The Regional Municipality of Halton, Oakville, Ontario. 76 pp.

Region of Waterloo (1976) *The Regional Official Policies Plan*, The Regional Municipality of Waterloo, Waterloo, Ontario. 102 pp.

Revised Statutes of Ontario (1970a) *The Wilderness Areas Act*, Queen's Printer, Toronto. 2 pp.

References

Revised Statutes of Ontario (1970b) *The Provincial Parks Act*, Queen's Printer, Toronto. 9 pp.

Richardson, P. J. and J. McEvoy (1976) *Human Ecology: An Environmental Approach*, Duxbury Press, North Scituate, Massachusetts. 370 pp.

Rohrs, A. W. (1981) 'Open space zoning and the taking clause: a two-part test', *Missouri Law Review* **46**: 868–75.

Rose, J. G. (1974) 'A proposal for the separation and marketability of development rights as a technique to preserve open space', in V. G. Rose, *Legal Foundations of Land Use Planning*, pp. 279–96, Center for Urban Policy Research, Rutgers University, New Brunswick, New Jersey. 319 pp.

Schwartz, C. F., E. C. Thor and G. H. Elsner (1976) *Wildland Planning Glossary, General Technical Report RSW-13*, USDA Forest Service, Pacific South-West Forest and Range Experiment Station, Berkeley, California. 252 pp.

Searle, R. N. and M. E. Heitlinger (1980) *Prairies, Woods and Islands – A Guide to the Minnesota Preserves of the Nature Conservancy*, The Nature Conservancy, Minneapolis, Minnesota. 73 pp.

Seneca, J. J. and M. Taussig (1974) *Environmental Economics*. Prentice-Hall, Englewood Cliffs, New Jersey. 354 pp.

Sharrock, J. T. R. (1976) *The Atlas of Breeding Birds in Britain and Ireland*, British Trust for Ornithology, Beech Grove, Tring, Herts. 477 pp.

Sheail, J. (1976) *Nature in Trust*, Blackie, Glasgow and London. 270 pp.

Shivas, M. (1974) 'A brief history of the Hamilton Naturalists' Club', *The Wood Duck* **28** (4): 61–2.

Simberloff, D. (1976) 'Experimental zoogeography of islands: Effects of island size', *Ecology* **57** (4): 629–42.

Simberloff, D. S. and L. G. Abele (1976) 'Island biogeography: strategy and limitations', *Science* 193: 1032.

Simmons, I. G. (1978) 'National Parks in England and Wales', in J. G. Nelson, R. D. Needham and D. L. Mann, *International Experience with National Parks and Related Reserves*, pp. 384–409, Department of Geography Publication Series No. 12, University of Waterloo, Waterloo, Ontario. 624 pp.

Smyth, J. H. and I. A. Nausedas (undated) *Rural Lands and Landowners of Ontario: A Private Land Forestry Perspective*, Great Lakes Forest Research Centre, Canadian Forestry Service, Sault Ste Marie, Ontario. 97 pp.

Sprott, T. F. (1977) *Study of Environmentally Sensitive Areas*, Grampian Regional Council, Department of Physical Planning, Report to the Planning Property and Development Committee: 30 November 1977. 6 pp. (mimeo).

Stamp, D. (1969) *Nature Conservation in Britain*, Collins, London. 273 pp.

Stratton, J. (1979) 'Cover crops for pits and quarries', *Interface* **2** (1): 2–4.

Street, M. (1982) 'The Great Linford project: waterfowl research in a gravel pit wildlife reserve', in W. D. Svedarsky and R. D. Crawford, *Wildlife Values of Gravel Pits*, pp. 170–80, Miscellaneous Publication 17–1982, Agricultural Experiment Station, University of Minnesota, St Paul, Minnesota. 249 pp.

Sullivan, A. L. and M. L. Shaffer (1975) 'Biogeography of the megazoo', *Science* **189** (4196): 13–17.

Sutherland, D. A. (1981) *A Provisional List of the Rare Vascular Plants of the Regional Municipality of Halton, Ontario*, University of Waterloo, Waterloo, Ontario. 99 pp.

Svedarsky, W. D. (1982) 'The Red River Valley Natural History Area: wildlife management and environmental education in an abandoned gravel pit in north-west

Minnesota', in W. D. Svedarsky and R. D. Crawford, *Wildlife Values of Gravel Pits*, pp. 132–40, Miscellaneous Publication 17–1982, Agricultural Experiment Station, University of Minnesota, St Paul, Minnesota. 249 pp.

Swaigen, J. (1979) *Preserving Natural Areas in Ontario : Private Ownership and Public Rights*, Canadian Environmental Law Research Foundation Occasional Paper No. 1, Toronto, Ontario. 64 pp.

Swanson, G. A. (1982) 'Summary of wildlife values of gravel pits symposium', in W. D. Svedarsky and R. D. Crawford, *Wildlife Values of Gravel Pits*, pp. 1–5, Miscellaneous Publication 17–1982, Agricultural Experiment Station, University of Minnesota, St Paul, Minnesota. 249 pp.

Tans, W. (1974) 'Priority ranking of biotic natural areas', *Michigan Botanist* **13**: 31–9.

Tant, M. S., S. S. Varga, M. A. Fleming and M. A. Bryant (1977) *Biological Documentation of Natural Features in Regional Municipality of Halton*, Regional Municipality of Halton Planning Department, Oakville, Ontario. 74 pp.

Taoda, H. (1982) 'Urban forestry in the warm-temperate zone of Japan', in M. Numata (ed.), *Chiba Bay – Coast Cities Project*, pp. 71–81, faculty of Science, Chiba University, Chiba. 184 pp.

Temple, P. J. (1980) 'Plants of the Leslie Street headland, Toronto, Ontario', *Ontario Field Biologist* **34** (1): 19–32.

Terborgh, J. (1976) 'Island biogeography : strategy and limitations', *Science* 193: 1029–30.

Thompson, D., C. E. Murphy, J. W. Wiedel, F. W. Porter, C. A. Roswell and R. A. Harper (1977) *Atlas of Maryland*, Department of Geography, College Park Campus. University of Maryland. 116 pp.

Thurow, C., W. Toner and D. Erley (1975) *Performance Controls for Sensitive Lands: A Practice Guide for Local Administrators, Parts 1 and 2*, American Society of Planning Officials, Chicago, Illinois. 156 pp.

Tobias, T. N. and P. F. J. Eagles (1977) *An Environmentally Sensitive Area Management Study – Beverley Sparrow Field, Hyde and Rockton Tracts*, School of Urban and Regional Planning, University of Waterloo, Waterloo, Ontario. 85 pp.

Tokyo Metropolitan Government (1977) *Tokyo Fights Pollution*, Bureau of General Affairs, Tokyo. 222 pp.

Tramer, E. J. (1969) 'Bird species diversity : components of Shannon's formula', *Ecology* **50** (3): 927–9.

Trewartha, G. T. (1965) *Japan – A Geography*, University of Wisconsin Press, Madison, Wisconsin. 652 pp.

Udvardy, M. D. F. (1975) *A Classification of the Biogeographical Provinces of the World*, International Union for Conservation of Nature and Natural Resources. Occasional Paper No. 18, Morges, Switzerland. 48 pp.

Ukai, N. and N. L. Nathanson (1968) 'Protection of property rights and due process of law in the Japanese constitution', in D. F. Henderson, *The Constitution of Japan*, pp. 239–55, University of Washington Press, Seattle. 323 pp.

Whitcomb, R. F., J. F. Lynch, P. A. Opler and C. S. Robbins (1976) 'Island biogeography: Strategy and limitations', *Science* 193: 1030–32.

Yano, I. (1978) *Nippon – a chartered survey of Japan 1978/79*, Tsuneta Yano Memorial Society, Tokyo. 331 pp.

Yoshii, H. (1982), 'Environmental perceptions and beliefs of Chiba City residents', in M. Numata (ed.), *Chiba Bay – Coast Cities Project*, Faculty of Science, Chiba University, Chiba. 184 pp.

157

Index

Index

Pinus sylvestris 14
pollution 1, 14, 22, 50, 69
Powys County 94
Prince George's County 125
public participation 3, 20, 38, 41–2, 60–3, 72, 79

Quebec 111

rare species 1, 4, 8, 14, 45, 46, 50, 54, 56, 59, 60, 68, 76, 77, 86, 99, 105
Red Kite 55
restoration 80
Royal Botanical Gardens 81
Royal Society for the Protection of Birds 89
Royal Society for the Protection of Nature Reserves 90
Russia 100

Sand Lizard 86
Sassafras 142, 144
Sassafras albidum 142, 144
Sassafras Woods ESA 143–6
Savannah Sparrow 76
scale 5, 40, 44–5, 51
Scotland 56, 85, 86, 88, 89, 92
Scots pine 14
selection criteria 45–8, 51–9, 104, 133
Seto-Naikai National Park 108
Sharp productivity criterion 23
Sharp utility criterion 24
Sibley 82
Sites of Special Scientific Interest 46–7, 55–9, 81, 89–92, 98–9, 134
Snakeshead Fritillary 86
Song Sparrow 76
South Carolina 2
South Glamorgan County 94
South Korea 99
Sugar Loaf Mountain 94

taking issue 123–5, 130–2
technology 11, 20, 21, 26, 27, 36, 137–8
Tiburnon 124
Tokyo 109
Toronto 81, 113
transfer of development rights 123–5, 131–2

Union Gas Limited 78
United States 8, 43, 44, 47, 50, 72, 82, 91, 98, 110, 123–33, 134, 136–8

Wakayama 105
Wakayama Prefecture 85, 105–10
Wales 56, 85, 89, 90, 92–8
Washington, D.C. 125
Water management 3, 4, 40, 46–52, 60, 63, 69, 72, 74, 81–2, 108, 118, 125–6, 130
Waterloo 28
Waterloo Region 27, 81, 92, 113
Waterloo University 113
Whooping Crane 68
wildlife 1, 4, 6, 8, 30–3, 46, 52, 54, 55, 56, 60, 63, 68, 74, 76, 78, 86, 92, 103–5, 118, 123, 129
Wilfrid Laurier University 113
Windsor 68
Wisconsin 8, 123
Worcestershire County 93
World Conservation Strategy 3, 133
Wye Valley Area of Outstanding Natural Beauty 94, 97, 98

Yellow Mandarin 52, 53, 73
Yellowstone National Park 123
Yoshino-Kumano National Park 108

160